The Cry of the Eagle

By
Debra Hughey

Wake Forest, NC
www.scuppernongpress.com

The Cry of the Eagle
Debra Hughey

©2023 Debra Hughey

First Printing

The Scuppernong Press
PO Box 1724
Wake Forest, NC 27588
www.scuppernongpress.com

Cover and book design by Frank B. Powell, III

All rights reserved. Printed in the United States of America.

No part of this book may be reproduced or transmitted in any form or by any means, electronic or mechanical, including photocopying, recording, or by any information and storage and retrieval system, without written permission from the editor and/or publisher.

International Standard Book Number ISBN 978-1-942806-58-5

Library of Congress Control Number: 2023919178

Table of Contents

Forward iii
Chapter One, The Closing 1
Chapter Two, The Cabin 5
Chapter Three, The Chest 9
Chapter Four, Blue Sky Man 13
Chapter Five, Boy Babies 15
Chapter Six, Changing Times 19
Chapter Seven, To the Tensaw 23
Chapter Eight, Chocolate Chip Cookies 27
Chapter Nine, The Man Called Hawkins 31
Chapter Ten, Tecumseh's Talk 35
Chapter Eleven, To Pensacola 39
Chapter Twelve, A Creek Called Burnt Corn 43
Chapter Thirteen, A Talk with Bill 45
Chapter Fourteen, The Days Before Revenge 49
Chapter Fifteen, Fort Mims 51
Chapter Sixteen, Return to Talisi 55
Chapter Seventeen, After Mims 59
Chapter Eighteen, Holy Ground 63
Chapter Nineteen, Ole Hickory 67
Chapter Twenty, Broken Spirit 73
Chapter Twenty-One, Save My People 77
Chapter Twenty-Two, Ole Jackson, Face-to-Face ... 79
Chapter Twenty-Three, White Doe 81
Chapter Twenty-Four, The Journal 85
Epilogue 89
Photos 91
Acknowledgments 139

Painting of William (Billy) Weatherford which hangs in the Alabama Capital Building in Montgomery.

Forward

In this time of computers and smart phones, entire books are available online. Many people choose to read from these sources. In these changing times, subject matter is also different. History is not required at many universities and some of the most important events of our history are encouraged to be forgotten. If you prefer to read from your smart phone and do not like or know your history, then this book is not for you. On the other hand, if you want to hold a book in hand and enjoy reading about Native Americans who once called this land home, I think you will like *The Cry of the Eagle*. As with my other books, so that their story may be told, I have intermingled actual historical figures from the past with fictitious characters.

Come with me now, as we join Matthew and Jacob, two young men, who first appeared in *Just a Cotton Field* and *Dance With the Spirits*, as they learn firsthand about two of the most important men in Creek Indian History. In their quest to learn about these men, they once again experience the unexpected.

Chapter One
Estate Closing

Matthew Walker sat nervously in the attorney's office, looking at the Alabama Crimson Tide football pictures that covered the wall. Must be a big Alabama fan, I reckon, he thought to himself. He had arrived early for the appointment that he and his cousins had with Attorney Martin. The pretty, young secretary had told him to have a seat and as soon as the other parties arrived, Attorney Martin would see them. This was the day the estate of Aunt Minnie Raintree would be settled. Aunt Minnie Raintree, and she had insisted that she be called by her full name, was actually the great aunt of Matthew. She had suddenly passed away or walked the path of the Great Spirit as she would say the previous fall. Matthew and his friend Jacob had spent the weekend with her, and she had told them the story of their Native American ancestors.

It had been a wonderful experience and Mathew missed the one-hundred- and two-year-old woman tremendously. As Matthew's thoughts drifted back to that weekend, his cousins Marcus and Jonathan Walker arrived and the secretary ushered them into Attorney Martins' office, where more pictures of Alabama football players lined the wall.

Attorney Martin stood and greeted the Walkers and each one identified himself. As his cousins where much older than he, Matthew waited quietly until they had finished. Attorney Martin had noticed the young man eyeing the pictures on the wall and laughed as he said, "Auburn fan, are you?"

"Yes, sir, I'll graduate this summer from Auburn," Matthew said extending his hand.

"That's great! What's your major?" The attorney asked.

"Anthropology, with a minor in Southern History," Matthew answered with pride.

"Well then, that explains that. If you gentlemen will take a seat, we will get started," Attorney Martin said as he sat down in his huge brown chair and picked up a thick file. "Y'all are here today to settle the estate of Minnie Walker Harper."

"That would be Minnie Raintree Walker Harper," Matthew interrupted politely. "She would want that included sir."

"You are correct Matthew," the attorney answered smiling, thinking that he really liked this young man. "Mrs. Harper had amassed a large sum of money and property in her lifetime and she lived to be one-hundred and two, I believe. I understand she was quite a remarkable lady."

All three Walker cousins nodded in agreement. None of them had realized the financial status of their aunt as she had lived very modestly. At the end of the meeting, fifty-thousand dollars would be placed in the accounts of the two older men as well as that of Matthew's father, who could not attend the estate closing. Matthew would receive twenty-five thousand. Attorney Martin had smiled as he read the written words of Minnie Raintree Walker Harper. "To my great nephew Matthew, I leave my cabin in the cotton field. I know you love the old place just as I did. I know you feel the spirit of our ancestors, Soaring Eagle and Little Flower. I know you hear and will hear again the beating of the drum. Look in the old chest and you will find another journal that I intended to give you. I think you will find it very interesting. I love you Matthew. Please continue to listen for the drums and when you hear, look for me, I will be there." Attorney Martin handed the hand-written note from Aunt Minnie Raintree to Matthew. "I guess you understand her strange words."

"Yes sir, I do," Matthew answered, taking the note from the attorney, as he wiped tears from his eyes. He had never dreamed that Aunt Minnie Raintree would leave him money or the old cabin. "Thank you, sir."

"Oh, by the way," Attorney Martin said. "Here's the key to the cabin. I will prepare the deed for you in the next few days and the money should be in y'all's account by noon tomorrow. My fee and any other expenses have already been deducted from her account. This information is listed in the papers here," he said, giving each a copy from the stack. "Sure, been nice working for Aunt Minnie Raintree and for you folks. Good luck to you Matthew in the future and I hope you enjoy the cabin. Sounds like it's a special place for you." The attorney continued, wondering again about the strange words of the woman.

"It is a very special place. Thank you again sir," Matthew answered, shaking hands with the attorney. He could hardly wait to text his friend, Jacob to tell him the news. They would be spending much time at the cabin in the cotton field.

Chapter Two
The Cabin

The following day was Saturday and just as they had done a few months earlier, Matthew and Jacob packed enough clothing for the weekend and headed down the road in Matthew's old truck.

"Guess you can buy you a new truck now that you got some money'" Jacob said, laughing as he bounced around when Matthew hit a bump.

"Nope, like this old truck. It's just what I need. Think I will use part of the money to get my masters. You know that," Matthew answered as he pulled into the Walmart parking lot. "We've got to get food. Mom packed me some, but it won't be enough. You know Aunt Minnie Raintree won't be there to make us hot chocolate and cookies," Matthew paused, "This is going to be hard buddy. Don't make fun of me if I cry when we get to the cabin."

"I won't Matthew," Jacob answered. "I know how you feel. Shoot, I may cry too!"

It was amazing how the old lady had affected him, and he missed her as well. The cabin, on its own seemed to have a hold on them and he was happy that Matthew had inherited it.

After picking up the needed items at Walmart, the two young men continued down the road. Matthew seemed to be in deep thought and said very little, even turning the radio down when one of his favorite songs was playing. "Matthew," Jacob said hesitantly, "Are you okay buddy?"

Matthew smiled, "Yes, I'm good. Just thinking about the weekend, we spent with Aunt Minnie Raintree and the things that happened. Jacob, we both will soon have degrees in Anthropology. You know what we saw and heard is not supposed to happen."

"Scared me bad, Matthew," Jacob said softly. "Never told you how bad and I'm a little nervous now. I mean going back and all. Reckon we will experience that again?"

"Don't know if Aunt Minnie Raintree was responsible for that phenomenon or if it will ever occur again without her being here," Matthew answered, slowing down and turning his signal on. "But we are going to find out."

Both young men became silent and Matthew turned the radio off and rolled the windows down. The warm sunshine and quiet stillness instantly enveloping them as they drove down the tiny dirt road that led to the cabin that now belonged to Matthew.

A lump formed in Matthew's throat and his heartbeat faster as they rounded the last bend in the road and the cabin came into view. Spring weeds and grass grew in abundance crowding out the rose bush and flowers that Aunt Minnie Raintree had tenderly groomed. "Well, buddy, Matthew whispered, wiping the tears from his eyes. "Reckon we will need to do a little cleaning up. Glad I thought to bring a hoe and shovel. Ready to go inside?"

Jacob nodded, understanding the emotions his friend was experiencing. Matthew placed the key in the lock and the old wooden door slowly opened. The cabin looked spotless just as Aunt Minnie Raintree had left it and both young men expected to see her in the kitchen making hot chocolate and cookies.

"Oh, man," Matthew exclaimed. "Didn't expect to feel like this. Jacob, it's like she is still here."
"I know, I feel her presence too. Think I need to get some fresh air," Jacob answered as he bolted back out the door.

"Think maybe I do too," Matthew exclaimed, following his friend outside.

The two sat on the steps of the old cabin, quietly talking about the emotions they both were experiencing. "What do you think about us cleaning up this mess of weeds before we go back inside?" Matthew asked, standing up. "That will give us more time to settle down."

"Sounds good to me," Jacob answered, pointing to a doe and her two fawns, grazing on the green grass near the woods. "Just seeing the deer is settling to me."

"Yes, I feel better already. You want the hoe or the shovel?" Matthey asked, smiling as the mother deer looked up at them and then continued grazing, showing no fear.

"How about a weed eater?" Jacob laughed, knowing they did not have one.

After an hour or so, the little yard and flower bed looked neat and the pink rose bush was especially pretty. Both young men knew that Aunt Minnie Raintree would be happy. Grabbing cokes and sandwiches from the cooler, the two of them sat back down on the steps, enjoying the nice breeze that blew up from the river.

"Think we need to bring some lawn chairs and sit underneath the trees down closer to the river." Jacob said, wiping his mouth.

"Yeah, but we need to do some cleaning down there too," Matthew added. "Maybe we will do that the next time we come. Ready to go back inside? I want to see what I have. I told my cousins that their wives could get a few dishes and things like that."

This photo of an Elderly Creek Indian Woman is what the Author believes could reflect the appearance of Aunt Minnie Raintree.

Chapter Three
The Chest

The next few hours were spent going through the belongings of Aunt Minnie Raintree. Strangely enough, there seemed to be a sense of comfort and peace and both Matthew and Jacob were totally at ease, but still feeling the presence of the old woman.

"Looks like we've pretty much gotten things sorted out," Matthew said, not really wanting to part with anything that belonged to Aunt Minnie Raintree. "Save the old chest over there 'til last. I know that there will be some very interesting things inside." Matthew slowly opened the top to the old chest. "Oh, my goodness," He exclaimed. "Jacob, come look at this!"

Both boys starred in disbelief at an old picture of a beautiful young woman who was obviously Aunt Minnie Raintree. Around her neck were the tiny blue beads that she had so proudly worn. Beside the picture lay an envelope with the name Matthew neatly written.

"Matthew, she was so pretty," Jacob said softly. "Wonder were the beads are? Didn't you tell me that she was holding them when she was found in the cotton field?"

"Yes, she was," Matthew answered. "Wait a minute. Attorney Martin gave me another envelop at the estate closing and told me to open it later. It's still in the truck. I'll be right back," he said as he rushed out the door.

Matthew looked excited as he came back in the cabin. "There's something hard inside," he said breathlessly. "Do you think that …"

"Matthew, will you just open the envelope," Jacob said impatiently.

Matthew sat down in front of the old chest and slowly opened the envelop, the blue beads falling out into his hand. Tears slid down his checks as he clutched them to his chest. "Aunt Minnie Raintree," Matthew said softly. "Aunt Minnie Raintree."

"Matthew, don't you think you should open the envelop in the chest? It has your name on it too. "Jacob said, touching his friend on his shoulder.

Shaking his head, Matthew reached for the envelope and slowly opened it. "This is another letter from her," he said emotionally as he began to read.

"Matthew, my boy, what a wonderful time I had with you and Jacob. Oh, how I wish that I had more time to spend with you. I have much more to tell you about our people, but it is time for me to go. You see, I hear the drum beat and it is calling my name. Matthew, you will find a journal in the chest. It contains information about two important leaders of our people, Billy Weather and Peter McQueen. I found this tucked away inside of my mother's things. The story was passed down to my grandmother, Morning Star, by a close friend of our family, a white man known as Blue Sky Man. Blue Sky Man spent most of his life as a close companion to Billy and knew Peter quite well. This is the story of their courage and bravery, but mostly about their love for their people and this land, their home. Matthew, the drums are getting louder. I must go. I love you."

"Matthew," Jacob said softly. "Do you realize she wrote this note just before she went out into the cotton field and ..."

"Walked the path," Matthew finished. "Yes, I do, Jacob. This is amazing. She obviously was not sick or in any pain. Aunt Minnie Raintree, as she said, heard the call of the drums and she answered them."

"Matthew, I think I need to go back outside," Jacob whispered as he turned toward the door.

Matthew placed the folded note back in the chest and followed his friend. He felt lightheaded and needed some fresh air. "Oh, my goodness, Aunt Minnie Raintree."

Both sat down on the old wooden steps. Nearly an hour had passed and as if in agreement, neither spoke. They listened to the red bird calling his mate and the lonely sound of the whistle of the train rumbling down the track.

Suddenly Matthew stood up and shielded his eyes as they

looked across the cotton field. The brown cotton stalks looking like tiny soldiers in the bright afternoon sun. He turned and motioned for Jacob to follow him and started walking toward the field. Continuing in silence, Matthew led the way. He had no idea where in the field Aunt Minnie Raintree had gone to walk the path, but he knew he would feel her presence. He did. Matthew looked at Jacob, "Here, Jacob she was right here when she walked."

Jacob looked at Matthew bewildered. "How, can you know this?"

"Come closer. Stand right here beside me," Matthew whispered.

Jacob moved closer and suddenly gasped. "Oh, she was here. Aunt Minnie Raintree was here."

The young men looked at each other and both began to cry. "Matthew, how can we be experiencing this? What is happening?"

"The spirit of Aunt Minnie Raintree is strong, Jacob!" Matthew explained. "I think she has said goodbye and now we can move forward," Matthew smiled. "Buddy, I think that I'm hungry for pizza. What about us going into town and picking up one? Then we can get back to the journal and see what else is in the chest."

"Sounds good to me. How about two. I am really hungry," Jacob laughed. "I love this place. You know, I bet there are a few arrows in this cotton field too."

"We'll certainly check that out. Come on. The sooner we go, the sooner we get back to Billy Weatherford and Peter McQueen!"

An hour later, Matthew slowly opened the frayed leather journal and began to read the words of Blue Sky Man.

Chapter Four
Blue Sky Man

The old man leaned back in the cane-bottom chair, pushed his hat back and rubbed his startling blue eyes. Turning to the man beside him, he began to speak. "Name's Elijah, but most folks just call me Blue Sky Man. Ya' see, some Indians raised me up and they called me that cause of my blue eyes. Why, I remember it jest like it was yesterday. My Ma and Pa and me and my big brother was traveling down that new road, they called the Federal Road. We wuz jest passin' through. We camped down by a little crick. Oh, I guess is was 'bout sundown and Ma had started puttin' us some vittles in her big black pot. She told me and Sam, that wuz my brother, to go and fetch her some water. Well," the old man paused and wiped a tear that had trickled down his check. "When we wuz a head'n back to the wagon, we seed two mean, nasty-look'n men going toward the wagon too." He paused again, with a far off look in his eyes as if he was looking back into the past. "They shot Pa down straight off and threw Ma down on the ground. Sam, he started hollowing and ran to Ma. They shot him in the stomach. I was to a'scared to move. I jest watched everything that happened from behind a big log. They never knew I wuz there. They went through the wagon and took what they wanted and threw the rest in the fire. I remember seeing them take a bow and shoot arrows in my Ma, Pa and Sam. One of them said, that if anyone ever finds these nice people, they will think the Creeks did this, laughing as they walked away." The old man stopped talking, a great look of sadness covering his wrinkled face.

The man sitting beside him softly said, 'I am sorry. So, what happened next?'

"Well," Elijah answered. "Some time went by, don't know how long, but it was starting to get dark. I was cold and hungry and scared. The close by sound of a pack of coyotes scared me even more," he smiled, "Figured they would eat me. Wasn't long afore five, maybe six Indian warriors came. I remember one of them had a deer slung over his shoulder. They looked horrified at what they saw, and one said, this was done by white man, not Creek. They wuz talking mostly in Indian words and all I could make out was white man and Creek. My nose started inching, and before I could help myself, I let out a big sneeze." He smiled again and continued. "Well, afore I knowed it, they all wuz standing there looking at me and I wuz looking at them. I could tell right off they weren't gonna' hurt me none. One reached down and picked me up and wiped the tears from my face. Father another said, pointing to my family. I nodded and cried harder. Name, one asked, and I replied as brave as I could that my name was Elijah. He shook his head and said Blue Sky Boy and pointed to the sky.

They piled sticks and rocks on my Pa and Ma and Sam too. One of them picked me up and said home. They took me to their village called Talisi near a big creek they called Euphaube. I was given to the sister of one of the warriors. I later found out that she had jest lost her son that was about the same age as me and I was treated like her son. Sir, these people took good care of me and raised me up in their way. I became real good friends with the one called, Peter McQueen, and later with the one called Billy Weatherford. I know the real story about them and if we can go inside now and let me buy you a drink or two, then I will tell you about Peter and Billy."

Chapter Five

1780
Boy Babies

"Well, you see, I was only a little fellow myself when the two boy babies came into this world, but this here is the things I was told and the way I remember. The fall winds blew cool and the sounds of the soon to be night echoed along the stream called Okfuskee. The Talisi woman of the wind clan picked up her blanket and began to walk to the huti for women, the pain in her lower back became stronger. This was her third baby and she realized this was jest the beginning of what could be a long night.

The boy child would be born before the light of brother moon began to fade away. His father, James was the first white trader to live in the land of the Muskogee and he had declared the child's name would be Peter. Peter spent his childhood between Okfuskee Creek and old Talisi town. Peter was raised as a Muskogee, but also knew the ways of the white man very well.

In the next warm season after the birth of Peter, another child was born, near the junction of the Coosa and the Tallapoosa Rivers near Coosada Town. He too was of mixed heritage, being only one-eight Muskogee. His father was Charles, a Scott trader from Georgia and his mother was Sehoy, a princess she was, the third woman to have that name, also of the Wind Clan. His Creek family called him the Truth Maker. His white father's friends called him Billy Larney or Yellow Billy. He had the look of his Scottish father, his hair reddish blond, his eyes soft brown, not the deep brown of the other boys, and his skin was fair. His appearance was that of a white child, but his actions and abilities wuz that of a Creek. He was an excellent swimmer and hunter with both his bow and arrow and his rifle. He played the game of stick ball with the natural ability of a Creek boy. Why, from an early age he showed strength and leadership, but had no interest in obtaining any of the education of the white man.

Even though they were mixed bloods, both boys were raised by the families of their mothers and wuz considered Creek. Both new the ways of the white man. This would influence and change the lives of both Billy and Peter. In the time of black berries in their twelfth warm season, the boys met for the first time at council in Tuckabatchee Town. Course I was right there with Billy," Blue Sky Man said happily. "The Creeks, they always looked at me kinda' funny like maybe they knew I weren't no Indian, but it didn't seem to bother them none."

'How is it that you knew both boys so well,' His companion asked?

"Well, ya' see, my Creek mother that took me in had family in Talisi and Coosada and we spent time in both villages.

"Anyway, back to the Tuckabatchee Council. Our age required us to set behind the warriors in the big circle near the old council tree. The talks of the chiefs and the headmen became long and tiring and us boys along with others our age slipped away. The old chief saw us and smiled. He musta' remembered that in his youth he done the same thing. This is the what happened next"

"Peter eyed Billy as they walked away from the council. He told me later that he wondered how someone with white skin and hair that shines red in the sunlight could be called a Creek. Peter called out to Billy in the Muskogee tongue," 'You! What name?' "And Billy replied, not liking the way he was being looked at or the tone use by the boy opposite him," 'I am Billy, what name you go by?' "Then Peter said with a smirk," 'I am called Peter.' "Peter pulled two chunky stones from his beaded pouch at his waist and yelled," 'bet I beat you at game.'

"Billy nodded, taking one of the chunky stones from Peter. The other boys with us devid up. Some on the side of Peter and the others on the side of Billy." 'I roll first,' "Peter said, in a tone of haughtiness," 'then take belt from you when I win.' "Peter bent his legs, one arm behind his back and threw the chunky stone. The stone began to roll at a quick pace, then hitting a pebble, flipped over, not going as far as Peter had intended. He knew it was not a good throw, but the expression on his face did not change as he watched Billy, as he got ready to throw his stone. Billy looked at Peter and smiled as the stone slid from his hand, rolling much farther than Peter's had before coming to a stop."

'I take pouch from you,' "Billy said, pointing to Peter's belt."

'No,' "Peter answered." 'You saw my chunky stone hit that rock. We roll again.'

"Billy just looked hard at the other boy and smiled again, shaking his head in agreement as he retrieved the stones and handed one to Peter." 'I roll first, then take moccasins and pouch from you,' "Billy told his foe." "Billy rolled his chunky stone and smiled as it rolled farther than the first. Peter then threw his and it stopped just short of Billy's."

'I take pouch and moccasins now,' "Billy said, turning to look at Peter with humor gleaming in his eyes."

"Embarrassment covered Peter's face but was quickly replaced with contempt as he began to remove his moccasins." 'There is no honor in taking moccasins. Have no need for pouch,' "Billy said as he again retrieved the chunky stones and handed them back to Peter." 'Maybe we meet again, in different game.' "The two boys eyed each other real cold like and Billy turned and begin to walk back to the council. He knew his uncle would be looking for him."

'Wait,' "Peter called out again." 'Who are you?'

"Billy turned and faced Peter again." 'I am Bill Weatherford.'

"Peter smiled," 'Ah, William Weatherford. I am Peter McQueen,' "He said as the two clasped arms in the way of Muskogee men. Both knew of the social and wealth status of the other's family. It was very clear that neither boy liked the other very much, but a sense of respect was formed between them." Blue Sky Man paused as though looking back into the past before he continued. "Peter and Billy had no idea that their futures would be bound together, and the fate of their people would be in their hands."

Chapter Six
Changing Times

Blue Sky Man cleared his throat and took a sip of his drink. "As time went by the old chiefs and shaman noticed the changes in the Creek people and their way of life as more white traders moved into the Creek land. They brought with them guns, the iron axe and cooking pots and also the cheap trinkets the Creek people valued as treasures at first, then as things they had to have. The Creek hunters were going farther and farther away from the towns and villages to hunt for the deer the traders wanted in exchange for the items of the white man. More often than not, these traders with their red hair and fair completion took the pretty Creek women for their wives. A change was taking place and not just the way the Creek people lived and looked but even their culture. Even I could see that," Blue Sky Man lamented.

"The items from the traders made life easier for the men and the Creek women enjoyed the colorful beads and blankets and each one had to have the little looking glass so they could see their reflection in the shining object. In time, they would look back and yearn for the days of the grandmothers. The looking glass could not predict their future."

* * * * * * *

"On this day, there was nothing to worry about. Billy and me, along with others had made the journey the day before to the Talisi Talwa. There was much excitement as there would be a Little Brother of War game between the Talisi warriors and those of Coosada Town. This would be the first game the two towns had played in several seasons. The players from both towns had gone through the required preparations and were ready to play the game which was scheduled to begin when the sun reached the midpoint in the sky. Men, women and the children not only from Talisi Talwa, but from towns from miles around had all gathered at the ball ground. Bets had been made and the exhilaration had continued to heighten. Everyone was ready for the game to begin. The crowd was silent with the beating of the drum and the Talisi chief walked to the center of the ballfield."

'Greetings,' "The chief announced in his loud voice." 'Welcome to Talisi Town. On this day the ball players of this town will take on the players of Coosada Town in a game of Little Brother of War. Rules will be followed and any player not obeying will be removed from the game. Mvto, (thank you), please enjoy the game.'

"The chief left the field and the shrill sound of a bone whistle filled the air. The ball game players began to enter the field from their hidden place behind the tree line. Those from Talisi on one side and the Coosada on the other. Wearing only breech clouts and moccasins, their bodies painted bright yellow, black and red, as if they were going to war. The opposing team players silently took their places, lining up facing each other. Billy told me that I had to watch. He said that I was too skinny and that my bones would break. I didn't like that at all." Blue Sky Man smirked. "I think the real reason was that I was a white boy and Billy, he was afraid the Creek players would try to hurt me, on purpose. Now, back to the game."

"Gripping his stick tightly, while awaiting the next whistle, Billy recognized the player across from him. It was Peter McQueen. They had attended the same event and many councils over the years since their first chunky game. Both still remembered the feeling of animosity that had developed between them."

"A large red tail hawk sailed down low over the ball ground; the screeching cry was heard by all. This was considered a good omen by the Talisi people and they roared in excitement as the referee blew the bone whistle again and threw the deerskin wrapped ball high in the air. Players on both sides ran in pursuit with a player from Coosada being the first to secure the ball. The Coosada players running alongside the ball carrier as the Talisi players all converged, attempting to take the ball away. This sequence continued for hours with first one team having the ball and then the other. All the players were streaming with sweat mixed with blood and several had limped from the ball ground in pain. One player from Coosada had to be carried from the field, his arm hanging limply at his side. The score was tied with both teams placing the ball between the other's goal four times. The first team to reach five would be declared the winner. The ball was pitched high in the air again and this time a young warrior now known as Talmus-Hadjo, Peter McQueen, secured the ball between his sticks. He lunged ahead of the other players and was nearing the goal when suddenly he felt pressure against his leg. He fell to the ground, the ball flying from the pocket of his stick into that of Billy Larney. Billy turned, then ran untouched in the opposite direction and cast the ball over the goal. The Talisi team had lost on its own ballfield. The humiliated players scowling as the players from Coosada yelled profanely and showed their contempt for the Talisi players, forgetting that the game was supposed to be one of entertainment and fun." Blue Sky Man paused and smiled as if he had just witnessed the game again. "Well, Billy Larney was the player who had cast the winning goal. He was the first to return to the center of the field, congratulating the Talisi players on a game well played and calming down the emotions of both teams. He then walked toward Peter and extended his arm. Peter glared at Billy, then smiled and placed his arm on that of the other warrior." 'Bill, you have beat me again. Is there no contest that I can defeat you,' Peter asked as he wiped the blood from his lip? 'After we recover and rest from the game, my people have prepared food and there is plenty for all. When brother sun begins to fall below the horizon there will be dancing.' He laughed, 'for those that are able, that is. I have friends you should meet and the Talisi king has words to share with our brothers from the Coosa.'

    Blue Sky Man smiled again saying, "food was shared, and the dancing and laughter continued until brother moon was high in the night sky. The outcome of the game was forgiven and the Talisi players vowed that victory would be theirs when the next game was played again in Coosada."

Chapter Seven
To the Tensaw

Blue Sky Man stopped for a minute as he recalled the events of so many years before. "By the early 1800s the Métis families had obtained wealth and became leaders in the Creek towns. Billy Weatherford was one of them and found it beneficial to be allowed to move in and out of both the Creek and white world. In early spring, Billy made the trip from Coosada down the Alabama River to the Tensaw/Little River region to visit with family members. Dressed in the attire of the white man, Billy looked the part, his light brown hair shinning in the sun. He arrived at the home of his brother-in-law, Sam Moniac right about supper time. The family had just sat down to eat when Billy knocked on the door of the large cabin. 'Bill, Bill come on in,' Sam proclaimed. 'You are just in time for supper. Betsy fetch another plate for your brother.' "Seeing me, Sam said, 'make that two plates, I see Bill has his friend with him.' You see, most folks knew that me and Billy spent a lot of time together. I just smiled and mostly listened, less someone spoke to me. Seeing her brother, Betsy squealed in delight," 'Billy, oh Billy, it is so good to see you,' "she exclaimed, hugging her brother." 'You are in luck, we're having your favorite, beefsteak and gravy.'

'Sam, Betsy, I too am happy to see you and the steak was just what I would like.' "Billy said, retuning the hug of his sister. Realizing that another young lady was already seated at the log table, he paused, instantly recognizing her as the pretty sister of Sam."

'Oh! Excuse me Miss Polly. I did not see you,' "Billy said, remembering that she had not so long ago lost her husband."

'Hello, Billy,' Polly said, smiling, 'it is good to see you again!'

"Well," Blue Sky Man said. "Billy returned her smile as he took the plate of steak and gravy from his sister and sat down next to Polly, thinking how pretty she looked. After the meal was finished, Bill, Sam and me went outside and sat on the wooden bench, beside the cabin. We sat in silence, listening to the sound of the slow-moving river and the occasional screech of the owl, then the far-off cry of the bobcat. Sam, not only the husband of Billy's sister was also his best friend, next to me, of course," Blue Sky Man laughed.

'Bill, how is everything up in the Creek Nation.'

'Sam,' "Bill answered slowly, puffing on his pipe. "'I do not know. At times I think that my people and the white man can live together in harmony. The one or the other does something that makes the other mad, and here we go. And Sam, you know that more and more white people are moving closer to or even into the Nation. I worry about what will happened and it very well may be soon.' "Sam knew that Bill aligned himself with the people of his mother. While living mostly as a white man and being only one-eight Creek."

'I was afraid of that Bill,' Sam answered. 'Many more white families are settling here along the river too. They know that this is mainly a Métis community and so far, there has not been any trouble. I too fear that the calm will not last.'

"The friends finished smoking their pipes and retired for the night as brother moon slid up over the treetops and the menacing cry of the bobcat followed the lonely call of the owl."

"Billy and me remained with his sister and brother-in-law for several weeks. He enjoyed being with his sister and talking with Sam. He also spent much time in the company of Miss Polly, as he called her. Told me to busy myself helping around the farm at these times, he did." Blue Sky Man smiled as he continued. "Both Sam and Betsy recognized signs that the two were becoming fund of each other."

"Sam and Bill and me while on an early morning ride to check on the small herd of Sam's beef cows had stopped by the river to water the horses. Sam, always saying what was on his mind, suddenly blurted out to Bill, 'So, when will you asked her?'

'Ask who what?' Bill answered in confusion.'

'Why, ask Polly to marry you!' Sam said laughing.

'How do you know that I want to ask her?' Bill asked, smiling at Sam.

'Just do. And so, does your sister and Blue Sky Man here. Think you will have a Creek ceremony. You know Betsy and Polly are already making plans.'

"Bill and Polly were married in the way of the Creeks two weeks later under a brilliant sunny sky. The Métis community had all turned out for the celebration. And as usual there was much eating and dancing. Some of the old ones had sat in the shadows of the big oak trees and talked of the future, shaking their heads in sadness. Bill had not planned on finding a wife, but he had. A few days after the celebration, he and his new wife and me made the trip back up the Alabama to Coosada."

"Along about the same time, in Talisi Town, Peter McQueen also took a wife, Elizabeth Durant. She, like the wife of Peter's adversary friend, Bill, came from a prominent Metis family. Both families chose to live in the way of the Creek."

"For the next several years, Peter and Bill live a time of happiness. Three children were born to Bill and Polly, two boys and a little girl that Bill had insisted would be named Polly. Then on a cold rainy night, the happy times for Bill would be cut short when his beloved wife, Polly suddenly took sick with a disease of the white man and walked the path to the Great Spirit. Family members would help raise the children. Bill would spend his time between Coosada Town and the Tensaw region. Peter too had children in Talisi Town. Both men became prominent leaders among their people. With the continued increase of white families moving closer to Creek land, the mood of the Creek people became tense and unsettled. The old ones predicted of the dark, difficult time looming ahead."

****

Chapter Eight
Chocolate Chip Cookies

Matthew closed the old journal and glanced at this cell phone. "My goodness, Jacob, its ten-thirty. We've been sitting here for over three hours. This is amazing!"

"Yeah, all first-hand personal history, I can't believe it! What a stroke of luck that Aunt Minnie Raintree was able to preserve it," Jacob said, yawning.

"Let's finish that pizza and then go out and stretch our legs for a while before we go to bed," Matthew said, placing the book on the countertop." I'm starving!"

"Sounds good to me. Sure, wish we had some of Aunt Minnie Raintree's chocolate chip cookies," Jacob answered.

"Me too, buddy," Matthew replied sadly.

The cool night air was refreshing as they stepped out on to the little porch, the moon shining brightly over the cotton field that had not yet been planted for the spring. Both young men were quiet as the sounds of night engulfed them. First the chilling sound of the coyote pack that ran across the field and then the sad forlorn call of an owl. Sounds both of them had heard many times before but seemed almost surreal here.

Jacob was first to break the silence. "Matthew, do you think that we will. …"

As if reading his friend's mind, Matthew answered, before Joseph could finish. "I don't really know what to expect here, but in my heart, I feel like they will come again, maybe not tonight or next month or even next year, but they will come."

"Do you think we should discuss this event with Professor Harris," Jacob asked as they sat down on the steps?

"No, he would think we were crazy and probably kick us out of his class," Matthew replied. "And you know, Aunt Minnie Raintree told us never to mention this to anyone. That we were privileged to witness the spirits of her, and my ancestors."

"Yeah, you are right," Jacob paused. "But what about the

girls? You know they're going to want to come here with us."

Matthew nodded in agreement, smiling when he thought of what Amber and Meg, their girlfriends for the past two years, would think if they told them. "Let's not worry about that right now. Hey, want to walk down the dirt road a ways? There is plenty of moonlight."

"Sure, why not," Jacob answered as they stood up. "Do you want walk out to the place where …"

"No," again knowing that his friend was referring to the place where Aunt Minnie Raintree had walked the path. "No, think down the road will be good," Matthew said softly. "Maybe we can hear the bobcat again."

They had not walked far from the little cabin when the blood-curdling scream of the bobcat stopped them in their tracks. "whew, maybe this is far enough," Jacob said. "The cat must be really close."

"Look, there he goes! Did you see him as he ran into the woods," Matthew asked, breathlessly?

"Yep, I saw him. Wait, what's that other sound?" Jacob asked as the soft beat of a drum suddenly filled the night air.

Both froze as the drumbeat got louder. Their eyes were drawn to a glowing light in the field and then, they saw them. Two men and three women dressed as the Creek people would have dressed over two-hundred years ago. They danced round and round the now apparent fire light singing chants from a different time. Matthew and Jacob stared in disbelief. Then, as suddenly as they had appeared, they were gone. One of the women paused briefly and seemed to smile before she vanished.

"Aunt Minnie Raintree," Matthew said in a whisper. "That was Aunt Minnie Raintree."

"I, I know" Jacob said softly. Matthew, I know.

They stood quietly in the little dirt road, staring into the darkness, where only seconds before, spirits from the past had danced before them. They had heard the drumbeat; saw the fire light and they had seen them. They had seen Aunt Minnie Raintree.

Matthew began walking with Jacob right behind him. Neither spoke, hearing only the yep of the coyotes and the hoot of the owl as they went back inside the cabin. It was now well past midnight, and both were exhausted from the long day and from the emotions of what they had just experienced.

"Jacob, do you want milk and some of these Walmart cookies before we go to bed? I can't talk about this now, but I feel a strange sense of peace."

"Me too," Jacob answered smiling slightly. "Sure, do wish the cookies were made by Aunt Minnie Raintree," he said again.

When Jacob woke the following morning, Matthew was already outside, sitting on the little steps. "Hey Matthew, you okay," Jacob asked?

"Yes, I'm okay," Matthew answered, sipping his coffee. "Just totally confused. Grab you a cup of coffee and come on out. It is beautiful out here. Just listen to the mourning dove."

Jacob was soon by Jacob's side with his coffee cup in hand. "You are right. Don't think I've ever been in more peaceful and beautiful place."

"Jacob," Matthew began slowly. "We are both rational and intelligent and we were totally sober last night. For the life of me, I can't figure this out. How is it possible to experience this phenomenon?"

"Got me on this," Jacob replied, looking out into the field. "But I tell you one thing for sure, we saw what we saw."

Matthew nodded in agreement. "Thought we might go into town and get a biscuit, but if its okay with you, I'd rather just have a pop tart and some more coffee," he said standing up. "Want to get back to the journal and read all we can before we head back up the road."

"Agree, totally," Jacob answered happily. "Let's stay out here to read. You get the journal and I'll get the pop tarts. I want the chocolate!"

****

Chapter Nine
The Man Called Hawkins

Blue Sky Man continued, "Benjamin Hawkins, and I tell you right now, I did not like this man. He had lived among the Tuckabatchee and Talisi people, traveling between the two towns and his Flint River home for several years. He had introduced himself as an agent for the great white father and that he had come to help. He came to make the lives of the Creek people better and to show them how to live as their white neighbors lived. Life would be much better he said. He would bring them farm animals, cows and pigs and show them how to plant as the whites did. They would then be able to grow more food and would not need to hunt for the deer. The women could learn to use the looms and make their clothing. All of this would be good he had said. The grandfathers had warned from the beginning that Mr. Hawkins and his better way of life for the Creek people was not good. It would, in fact, destroy their way of life and even destroy them.

Some of the people, especially the women, accepted the new ways, their life was after all easier. Many of the men, not having the need to hunt as often to supply food for their family, had become lazy and spent much time smoking their pipes and drinking the firewater of the white man. This was the seed for future times of discontent. The prediction of the grandfathers had been true, the way of life for the Creek people had changed and the white man with their families were coming closer and closer to the fire light of the Creeks."

Blue Sky Man paused again as if seeing the image in his mind. "The old council tree had been the site of many talks and councils over the years and now, in the early fall in the year of 1811, the biggest one of all would take place. Word had quickly spread, and thousands of native people would come to Tuckabatchee to hear the words of the great Shawnee leader, Tecumseh. Tecumseh considered himself among family as his mother had been born and had lived along the banks of the Tallapoosa.

He and his group of followers included the profit Seekaboo, who was also of Creek origin, arrived in great fanfare.

The huge crowd of Creek Warriors, including me and Billy and of course Peter and those from other tribes sat in amazed silence as the group led by the Shawnee leader entered the square ground of Tuckabatchee. They were dressed only in breech clouts and moccasins, their bodies painted black, their faces menacing. They looked like a bunch of devils, they did. After walking around the square ground and blowing smoke from his pipe, Tecumseh slowly walked to the Tuckabachee Chief, Big Warrior. He stood in front of the chief in silence as if demanding respect. Big Warrior starred back in defiance." Blue Sky Man laughed, "I admired Big Warrior for that.

As it had happened many times before, Billy and Peter, as prominent warriors among the Creek, found themselves sitting beside each other. Neither knew the events they were about to witness would be the making of history." 'What do you think, Billy?' Peter whispered as the two leaders before them continued to glare at one another.

'This Tecumseh is even more impressive than I thought,' Billy whispered back.

'Yes, he is,' Peter answered. 'Other than the slight limp he has, I have never seen such a show of strength,' he smiled. 'I think the Big Warrior is just a little intimidated.'

"Me, now, being white remember. I didn't trust this Tecumseh fellow at all. I just figured he was here to cause trouble. Billy and Peter as well as the hundreds of warriors who had gathered to hear the talk of the Shawnee leader, were disappointed. Several days would go by with Tecumseh refusing to speak, saying that the sun was too high, or it was too low.

In the meantime, Benjamin Hawkins talked of the plans of the great white father to enlarge the trade path that ran through the Creek Nation. This would allow for mail to be distributed from one part of the country to the other, he had said, not fully explaining that this would bring more white setters to and near the Creek homeland. Once again Hawkins had said, this would be good for the Creek people. The old ones had prophesied a bad outcome for the Creek people and as before, their words would be true. The new path became the Federal Road and the white people came by the thousands."

Chapter Ten
Tecumseh's Talk
1811

"The day finally arrived when Tecumseh declared he would give his speech. He would talk when the sun was at its midway point in the sky. All men with white skin would be banished from the town. Me, of course, was allowed to stay. Hawkins, tired of waiting, had already left for his home on the Flint River. He had informed the Creek people that the new road would be built through their nation and they would have no say in the matter.

The Creek chiefs and warriors were already upset by Hawkins when they gathered to hear the words of the Shawnee leader, making many of them more open to what he would say. As on the day of his arrival in Tuckabatchee, Tecumseh and his group of warriors entered the square ground with great fanfare. They were dressed as they were earlier, and the same ceremony was observed. Well, don't you know, that I was just as impressed as the Creeks were, but I still didn't trust him, not one bit. Well, Tecumseh, he slowly walked to the center of the square ground, every eye focused on the impressive man. Only the roaring sound of the upriver rush of water as it rolled over the great falls was heard as the light wind blew the gold and yellow leaves softly to the ground.

He stood looking out over the huge group of Indians, all dressed in the various ways of their tribes, not only the Creeks, but the Cherokee and Choctaw, the Shawnee and others he did not recognize." 'My brothers,' the Shawnee leader said softly. Then again loud and strong, 'My brothers, I have come to the land of my mother's people to warn you of the dangers of the white man.' "Seekaboo, the profit, standing by the side of Tecumseh, translated the Shawnee tongue of the Creek.

The sun had dipped low in the sky before the Shawnee completed his heartfelt talk. He had implored the Creek and the other tribes of the southland to join with the Shawnee. To come together as one people to stand against the white man and their families who were rapidly infiltrating the home of the Creek and the Cherokee. The speech had been passionate, his emotions ranging from tearful to that of raw anger. Many times, the talk was interrupted as the warriors surrounding Tecumseh, their clubs high in the air, yelling the battle cry of the wild Indians.

When at last, the talk was over, many of the warriors agreed to join with the Shawnee leader and become a part of his movement to join all Indians together as one. The Cherokee leaders had shaken their heads in disagreement and vowed to return to their mountain homes. The Big Warrior said, much to the dismay and total disagreement of his warriors, that the Creek people would live in peace with the white man. These words from the Creek chief would further widen the rift that had already formed among the Creek people. Including those that would comply and accept the white way of life and those that would fight to retain the Creek way.

Peter had excitedly waved his war club and Billy had done so, only half-heartedly. He wanted what was best for his mother's people, but at the same time, he did not want war to come to them. A war, he feared they could not win." Blue Sky Man continued, "I recall the conversation between the two warriors and later with Chief Big Warrior.

'Bill,' Peter had said, 'I agree with Tecumseh, but you do not. Why is that? Is the feel of your white blood stronger than that of your red,' Peter asked with a glint of insolence that had followed the man from his childhood?

'No, Peter,' Bill answered calmly, 'my red blood is the blood of my heart. I fear for all people, Peter. I have been to the big towns of the white man. There are more of them than the leaves on the oak tree in the forest. Peter, if we make war on the white man, they will destroy us, all of us.'

'Bill, I think that you have no courage to fight the white man,' Peter said sarcastically as he joined the large group of warriors that soon would be called Red Sticks.

"Tecumseh and his followers would stay among the Creeks at Tuckabatchee for several days. The Creek warriors learned the Dance of the Lakes and prepared to join with the Shawnee leader. Tecumseh had predicted that before he left for his Ohio home, the night skies over Tuckabatchee would be filled with light that stretched from one horizon to the other. The Tuckabatchee people had starred in wonder as the night sky was as bright as day.

Tecumseh again stood before the Tuckabatchee chief. 'Big Warrior, you do not believe in me. You do not know that I speak the truth. Did you not see the light that covered your town?' The two men looked at each other with contempt.

'Tecumseh, the plans you have will be the cause of many Creek people to perish. You will have the blood of my people on your hands.' Big Warrior said with anger in his voice. 'Again, I tell you that the Creek people can and will live in peace with our white brothers!'

'Big Warrior,' Tecumseh answered in anger, placing his hand on his knife. 'You are a coward. I will leave your town now and when I return home, I will stomp my foot and the houses of Tuckabatchee will fall to the ground.'

"Tecumseh left Tuckabatchee Town and continued gathering followers who supported his movement to save the red race from the white man. On his return to the Ohio River Valley, he paused and stomped his foot on the frozen ground. At that exact moment, the people in Tuckabatchee were awaken from their sleep as the ground began to roll and their houses fell to the ground. My friends, I remember Tecumseh's visit to Tuckabatchee as if it were yesterday."

Chapter Eleven
To Pensacola

"The next several months were filled with turmoil and the Creek people watched as more and more division occurred between them. Towns, as the people themselves, were now classified as white peace towns or red war towns. Most of the towns along the Tallapoosa and Coosa Rivers were affiliated with the Red Stick warriors. There were exceptions as Tuckabatchee, still under the influence of Big Warrior, was a peace town, while the across the river town of Talisi was a red strong hole. Peter McQueen assumed the position as the Red Stick leader.

It was the little things at first, some of the young warriors, many trying to prove themselves, would raid the white settlers living near the Creek land. An old horse would be taken or maybe a cow, the warriors leaving victorious. Then, the next time, the white man would fire shots at the raiding warriors, and they would fire back leaving the man with a Creek warrior's arrow deep in his arm, blood-soaking his homespun shirt.

The white settlers were nervous and becoming more and more frightened of the Creek people and of what could happen. Never stopping to think that maybe they, themselves, were encroaching too close to the homes of the Creeks and in some cases, actually building their cabins on Creek land. What right, some had said, did the red skin people have to live on the land that the white man wanted and intended to have. It mattered not at all that this was the land of the red people and had been for thousands of years.

So it was, the little raids had grown into big ones. Cabins were torched, white men were slain, with their wives and children, watching in horror. Such behavior would not be tolerated. The white man demanded justice and militias were formed to defend these people who now considered themselves victims of the red savages as they were now called.

The rift which had begun years ago had now widened

among the Creek people themselves, those who wanted to accept the white man and the new way of life and those who wanted only to live in the traditional way of their ancestors. So, what began as civil war between the Creek people now would escalate into one with both their own people as well one with the white man.

If battles were forthcoming, then Red Stick leaders knew more munitions would be needed. The Spanish in Pensacola had been on friendly terms with the Red Sticks, in fact embracing the movement and encouraging it. On a warm July morning in the year 1813, Peter along with Josiah Francis and High Head Jim and a large group of Red Stick warriors began the journey to the Spanish-held town. The trip would take several days from Talisi Town.

The Red Stick warriors thought it best that they split up, not traveling as one large group, but in smaller groups that would meet near Pensacola about the same time. Along the way, after having hard feelings with Métis plantation owner James Cornells, High Head Jim's group of Red Stick warriors attacked and destroyed his home, taking his wife Betty as captive." Smiling, Blue Sky Man continued, "fortunately, the ransomed lady was traded for a pretty blanket in Pensacola. When the Red Sticks converged near the large frontier town, Peter decided to make camp, to rest and finalize plans for the following day.

'Peter, do you think the Spanish governor will give us the munitions we need,' Josiah asked as he stirred the campfire?

'He will when I tell him the strength and number of our Red Stick forces,' Peter answered, sitting down near the fire. 'Let's get some sleep now and be on the move before brother sun shines on us with the new day.'

High Head Jim on the other side of the fire quickly replied, 'the Spanish governor will give us what we ask if he knows what is good for him.'

"The Red Sticks arrived in the bustling town of Pensacola by midmorning and went immediately to the large building where government meetings were held. Only Peter and the two other leaders were allowed inside. The astonished party of Red Sticks waited outside; most had never been in a large town of the white man. The cobblestone streets were filled with men and women of different colors and races, all speaking in their native tongues. Most paid little attention to the Red Stick men, as it was common to see Creek and Choctaw warriors in the frontier town. Three men, standing on the corner of the busy street did pay attention, close attention.

I, of course, was told to wait outside and saw these men as they talked but did not hear their words. Things would have been different if I had," Blue Sky Man shared, sadly as he continued the story.

'That's the group we were told to be on the lookout for,' a seedy-looking man said to one of the others who was neatly dressed and sported a stylish top hat and holding a cane.

'Yes, we will be on the watch and see what their actions are. One of them is that scoundrel Peter McQueen. I know he is up to no good. When we get the information we need, and they are on their way back to Mississippi Territory we will make our report. Our job is to let the captain know how many there are and how much munitions they have,' the man said, tipping his hat to one of the ladies of the street who walked by, her brightly-colored parasol bouncing over her painted face.

The Spanish governor, Gonzales Manrique, was waiting for the Creek men. He had briefly met them before and knew they were the most powerful, influential and dangerous of all the Red Stick leaders. 'Peter, Josiah, Jim,' he said. 'It is a pleasure to see you again.'

"Peter nodded his head in white man fashion." 'Yes, governor it is a pleasure to see you again. We will not waste your time, sir.' Peter continued. 'You do understand that the circumstances of my people require munitions, many munitions. You have indicated that the Spanish government will help us. We are here to get the guns and powder now.'

"The governor looked at Peter and smiled," 'I am aware of the situation of your people, but I am only allowed to give you a small, a very small amount of munitions,' he continued. 'I will give you gun powder and lead as well as food and blankets for your people, but no guns.'

"Peter told me later that he could have placed his knife in the governor's heart as both Josiah and Jim did reach for their knives on their belts. Peter glanced at his companions and shook his head. 'We need more, much more,' Peter replied in anger. "We will destroy this town. I have many warriors outside and thousands more who will destroy the white settlements between this town and the Tallapoosa, including those on the Tensaw.'

'As you wish Peter,' the governor answered, his voice cold and calculating. 'I will have militia on your warriors before you can load your muskets.'

"Peter realized the situation and nodded his head." 'Very well, we will take what you will give us and leave you.' "The two strong men looked at each other with respectful coolness and the three Creek leaders returned to the cobblestone streets where the munitions and food had been placed. The Creek warriors quickly loaded the pack horses and began the journey back to the Tallapoosa. The three men on the street corner silently watched and stealthy slipped away. They had the information they needed and would be paid handsomely."

Chapter Twelve
A Creek Called Burnt Corn

"Peter had divided his warriors along with the supplies into several groups using different paths. When the main group reached the Wolf Trail Crossing on Burnt Corn Creek, Peter realized the warriors needed to stop for a brief rest and to eat the remainder of their fried bread before making their way to the Tallapoosa.

The flat peninsula formed by the curve of Burnt Corn Creek made a good place to camp and the large pine trees offered shade from the hot sun. Peter motioned for the warriors to stop. Many of them had not yet reached the peninsula and were still out of sight in the deep woods. Peter sat down on a dead pine limb beside Josiah and reached into the pouch that hung by his side for the last piece of fried bread. 'It will be good to be back home in Talisi. My stomach makes much noise for deer and corn.'

Josiah laughed, 'I too am hungry. Peter, I know we did not get guns and enough powder. What is your plan for us to obtain more?'

The two men continued talking about the shortage of munitions. High Head Jim, who had been walking around the edge of the encampment suddenly gave the sign for silence. No guard had been posted.

The militia, that had been alerted by the spies in Pensacola, under the direction of Colonel Caller, with nearly one-hundred fifty men and thirty Tensaw Métis, had located Peter and his warriors. The Red Stick warriors were surprised by the militia when they stormed the camp. Fleeing into the thick cane break, the warriors avoided injury, but a Creek woman and a slave who were traveling with the group were killed.
Peter quickly took control and settled his warriors.

'These white men make poor soldiers,' Peter shouted to his warriors. 'Look at them, we are barely out of sight and yet they stop to take our supplies.' With the bone-chilling cry of a

Creek warrior, Peter led the Red Stick warriors out of the cane break. The white militia fled as more Red Sticks coming from other paths joined in the battle. Only a few soldiers remained to continue the nearly three-hour battle before they too withdrew. When the smoke of the battle had cleared, twelve Red Stick warriors had been slain and several of the pack horses, including the packs had been taken. The white militia had lost only two men with several wounded.

Peter smiled when his group of Red Sticks returned to the Tallapoosa and heard word that white militia Colonel Caller had lost his horse in the retreat and was lost in the woods for more than two weeks." A Métis from the Tensaw settlement found the scared hungry man and took him home. This, and the retreat was an embarrassment for the Tensaw militia. Peter and his warriors considered this a victory.

While plans were now underway for retaliation in the Creek Nation, the whites, blacks and Metis were filled with a sense of dread. They realized the Red Sticks had been embolden by the events at Burt Corn Creek and now were ready for the next move. They feared that move would be the Tensaw.

Chapter Thirteen
To Talk with Bill

"Peter, Josiah and High Head Jim sat by the fire in Talisi Town. I sat behind the warriors. I was always close by and they paid me no mind as they talked. All three were in deep thought about the plans that needed to be made. While Josiah and Jim were both strong, fearless warriors, both looked to Peter for wisdom. He seemed to know what the white leaders planned and was usually one step ahead of them.

As if he knew what they were thinking, Peter suddenly said, 'I did not have a lookout posted at Burnt Corn. That was a mistake. It will not happen again.' He had blamed himself for the death of his twelve warriors, twelve that he would need.

'Peter, we should have thought of that too,' Josiah answered. 'Things would have been worse if Jim had not heard the approach of the white militia.'

'I only heard them when they were on top of our camp,' High Head Jim replied. 'And they were making much noise,' he laughed. 'They were like a pack of the flop-eared hounds of the white man.'

Both Peter and Josiah joined in the laughter, the humor helping to lighten the mood, for a moment. Taking a deep breath, Peter frowned again. 'The white soldiers already know we will come to the Tensaw in revenge of the death of our warriors, but what they do not know is when,' he paused, staring intently into the fire. 'My scouts tell me that many white settlers, Métis, black men and even some of the friendly Creek people are flocking to the house of Samuel Mims. Their intention is to make the place into a fortress, a place of safety.' Peter paused, looking out over the Talisi village, smiling as he watched several young boys enjoying a game of chunky. 'I think this fort called Mims, will instead be a place of death for both the white man and the red,' he whispered in a voice as cold as the ice on the stream during the season of no leaves.

Josiah and Jim nodded in agreement. 'We are ready to

follow you Peter,' Josiah said. 'The land of the Creek must be preserved.'

'Do either of you know where Billy Weatherford is? He has homes, both at Hickory Ground and also near the Tensaw. I have not had words with him in many suns. I need to know where he stands on this matter.'

'My woman has family at Hickory Ground, I will talk with her,' High Head Jim said as he stood up. 'I will report to you when the sun rises.'

"I quietly moved closer to the fire and cleared my throat. I think, my friend Bill is at his home on the Coosa. Peter nodded to me and said that is good. The following morning, Jim was waiting at the square ground for Peter with the information he needed. Billy Weatherford is indeed at his plantation at Hickory Ground Jim said. The three warriors and me left immediately after the hearty morning meal for the Coosa River. Peter hoped to make the trip before the sun slid below the western horizon. We met several groups of Red Stick warriors along the path, all of them heading to Autossee. Both the town of Autossee and Talisi were among the main Red Stick towns. There was much planning to be done before the Red Stick party headed to the Tensaw. Peter had told them that he would be back in Talisi Town in two suns.

The three Red Stick leaders and me went directly to the home of Billy Weatherford when we arrived at Hickory Ground. Billy and his family had just finished their evening meal. He told his family to excuse themselves and asked the black woman who prepared his meals to bring food to his visitors. Bill looked at me and grinned, 'Well Blue Sky Man, how are you? It has been much too long since you were home,' Bill said showing the affection he felt for his close friend. You see, I spent my time with both Billy and my friend Peter. Bill then looked at the Creek men, who looked very much the part of the Red Stick warriors that they were and continued, 'Well Peter, Josiah and Jim, what brings you to Hickory Ground.

'Hello Bill,' Peter answered, sitting down at the long table that looked more like the table of a white man than that of a Creek. Peter told him what had really happened at Burnt Corn, not the version the white soldiers had given. 'We did lose twelve good warriors, but we took the victory. Bill, the white soldiers and their leaders ran off like a bunch of scared rabbits.' Peter smiled and continued, 'I heard that Captain Caller, the leader got lost and wondered around in the woods. It was two or three suns before he was found.'

When the meal of beef steak, potatoes and fried bread had been consumed, Bill and the Red Stick warriors move into a room where several soft chairs were arranged around the glass windows of a large room. Josiah nor Jim had said little during the meal. Looking around the nicely decorated room, Josiah coldly remarked in Creek, 'Bill Weatherford, why you live like white man? You think you better than Creek?'

Bill leeringly eyed Josiah and High Head Jim. He knew both men had accepted little of the white ways and were very capable of pulling knives from their beaded belts and slashing his throat. While he was not afraid of them, he did slide his hand a little closer to his own knife. 'No, Josiah,' he answered, 'but my family does like the comforts we have. I do spend much of my time in the woods down by the river.' He smiled before continuing, 'lets us go down and sit by the river now to talk. I think you will be more comfortable there.'

Peter nodded to Bill, realizing that he had defused a potentially bad situation. 'Yes Bill, I think that will be good.'

When the warriors and Bill and me walked the short distance to the river and sat down on the stumps that had been left near the slow-moving water, Bill turned to Peter. 'Now, Peter, tell me what the purpose of your visit is today. I know that you did not come here for small talk.'

'I will not waste time Bill,' Peter answered. 'I need to know where you stand. You know that after the big road the white government built through our land, more and more of them have moved closer and even into our nation. This movement will only get worse. The attack on me and my Red Stick warriors at Burnt Corn was an attempt to take from us weapons and supplies that we need. This is only the beginning of what will happened. Many white soldiers will come to our land and kill us, even our women and children. We must stop them now!' Peter finished with ice in his voice and fire in his eyes. 'My question for you is, my brother, which side will you choose, will you fight for your red people, or will you take up your knife against us?' Peter paused, 'or will you sit in your fancy white man cabin and do nothing?'

Bill was not surprise at the blunt questions from Peter. He saw the wild anger in his eyes, and glancing at Josiah and High Head Jim, saw pure hatred in theirs. He had spent much time thinking about this. He considered himself a Creek and were it not for his wife, who was part Creek herself, and his children, he would take up the red stick to proudly defend the people of his mother, Sehoy, and the Creek people. His wife had begged him to remain neutral and not get involved in the fight that was sure to come. Deep down inside, he knew she was right, and he had decided not to join with the Red Sticks.

He looked a Peter, preparing himself for the barrage of anger that would come from the Red Stick leader. 'Peter, I cannot take up arms against my Métis family and friends. It is their choice to join the way of the Creek and the white man together.'

Peter glared at him and the two Red Stick leaders at his side both pulled their knives from their belts. Bill calmly stood. 'My Red brothers, I think it best for you to leave. I have told you of my feelings and by decision.'

Peter indicated for his companions to put their knives away. 'Bill Weatherford, you will regret this decision.'

'Yes,' Josiah said, again speaking in Creek, his dark eyes flashing, 'not only will you pay, but your family will suffer!'

Bill looked at me and sadly said, 'My friend, I am afraid there will be many dark days ahead for my Creek family and the entire Creek Nation.'

Chapter Fourteen
The Days Before Revenge

"Many warriors joined the Red Stick leaders as they stalked angrily away from Hickory Ground. Soon final plans were underway by the leaders and bundles of broken sticks were sent to Red Stick towns. Each day that a stick was thrown away was a day closer to the day of retaliation. The warriors held a big war dance to ready themselves for the events that would soon occur. Afterwards, two groups headed for the settlements in the southern portion of the territory. Seven-hundred, fifty Red Stick warriors, with their red clubs waving high in the air, moved toward the Tensaw. Prophet Josiah Francis led a smaller group in the direction of the whites living in upper regions. Bill Weatherford had again received word from the war leaders, that his family would be taken hostage if he did not join in the movement against the whites. He had reluctantly given in to their demands, hoping that he could persuade them to at least spare the white women and children. He quickly was installed as one of the leaders of the large group of Red Sticks.

By light of the late summer moon, they traveled, taking paths through swamps that had been used by the Creek people for centuries. Ample amounts of corn left by the white settlers and Métis in their haste, supplied food for the warriors. Spirits were high and the prophets had promised success and that the Giver of Breath would provide safety for the Red Stick warriors.

Taking only a few days, the Red Stick warriors, arrived in the Tensaw area. Scouts had informed them the Métis, who had led the Burnt Corn attack, were indeed at the Mims farm. This is the story told to me later by one of the fortunate survivors.

Rumors of upcoming attacks on the Tensaw settlements had spread and both the whites and Métis had fled from their homes, to a place that would be known as Fort Mims. Most of the mass of people had made the small fort their home for nearly a month and living conditions were crowded and unsanitary.

Dysentery was rampant and many were sick. From time to time two or three would leave the fort and go back to their farms for food and supplies. Often Red Sticks would be spotted but this was quickly downplayed as just excited imagination by the military commander, Major Daniel Beasley. Beasley had sent a letter by a post rider to his superior, General Claiborne, that everything was fine at the Mims fort and it had not been any real Indians sighted.

Two negro boys, outside the Mims compound had again given the alarm that the Red Sticks were out there. 'But sir,' one had said. 'I's for sure I seed'em. They's wuz hollering and waving them Red Sticks.'

'What you saw,' Major Beasley answered, 'was some red cows grazing on the hillside.' Turning to the private by his side, he continued, 'have this boy flogged for his insolence.'

Major Beasley was tired. He had been cramped in a small space with over two-hundred and fifty scared whites, Métis, friendly Creeks and their blacks along with over one-hundred military personnel for weeks. Tomorrow would be Sunday, a day of rest and rest he would do. Wiping sweat from his face, he again turned to the private. 'Blast this heat. I can hardly breath. I'm going to my quarters,' he smirked, 'to rest. Bring me a bottle, no bring me two bottles of that corn liquor. I do not want to be disturbed. Unless there is a real Indian threat.' Major Beasley then retired to his quarters and drank the contents of both bottles.

The Red Sticks were indeed close, very close to this flimsy stockaded fort. They had come near enough to watch the people inside go about their miserable routine, some very carelessly. The Red Sticks also saw the sand that had accumulated around the bottom of the main gate and it would not close. They saw the Mims house and their outbuildings as well as the quickly thrown up shelters of the military. They were ready to avenge the death of their brothers and when the sun was high overhead the next day, it would be time.

Chapter Fifteen
Fort Mims

The date on the calendar of the white man was August 30 in the year 1813. The Red Sticks, wearing only loin cloth, their faces painted red and black waited patiently just out of sight of the fort. Many inside, were eating their noon meal, children were at play and an old man played his fiddle, the soft sweet sound filling the air. The military guards, totally oblivious to the red warriors, were engrossed in a game of cards. Suddenly from inside, the warriors heard a single drumbeat.

Thinking they had been sighted, Far Off Warrior gave the signal to attack. William Weatherford then gave his shrill war call that sounded like the *cry of the eagle*. The soldier that had been posted to stand guard heard the sound of running feet. Looking up, he saw the Red Sticks. 'Indians, Indians,' he shouted out. Quickly the yard surrounding the fort was quickly filled with warriors and their blood-chilling war whoop.

In confusion, pandemonium and fear, the military attempted to form a line of defense. Major Beasley ran from his cabin, unbelief and fear covering his face. As he opened the door, he felt the sharp pain of a barbed war club pierce his stomach. "I was told that," Blue Sky Man said, "that he was heard to say as he fell to his death," 'what have I allowed to happen?' Very soon, nearly half of the Mississippi Territory volunteers fell to the ground. Prophet Patty Welch had again promised that the bullets of the white man could not harm the Red Sticks. Welch and the other prophets had said that only a very small number would perish. He had danced around the fort waving his red war club, urging on the warriors.

Weatherford, having little faith in the prophets, watched as a militiaman took aim and fired, bringing Welch to his knees. Undaunted, the prophet continued yelling for the warriors now to drop the guns of the white men and enter the fort using the weapons of old. Billy yelled out to those around him, 'to throw away your weapons will mean certain death.' And just as quickly the warriors succumbed, lying lifeless beside their white enemy. A Métis himself, Dixon Baily, captain of the white and Métis militia had gained control of the northern wall of the fort. The Red Sticks, doing as William Weatherford had ordered, secured possession of the other side of the fort and was able to dispatch deadly fire through the firing holes.

The horrendous slaughter continued for over two hours. Both sides lost many. The militia and white inhabitants had gained a slight momentum with the women and older children helping in any way they could. The Red Stick warriors withdrew from the fort to plan their next move and gathered around William Weatherford and the other leaders. Weatherford. Looking back toward the fort was the first to speak. 'We have done what we came to do. We have killed many and we have lost many of our brave warriors, too many. We should now leave and go back to our homes.

'To leave this place now would accomplish nothing. Many of the Métis who have abandoned the Creek way still live,' a Red Stick leader declared.

'I know the Métis Baily still lives. I will not go from here as long as the sun shines on him,' another said, wiping blood from his arm.

Most of the Red Stick warriors agreed and had worked themselves into a frenzy. 'Kill the whites, kill the Métis, kill them all, a tall warrior, his face painted red had screamed out. Blue Sky Man paused, his voice shaking, "I was standing beside Bill when he turned to Peter and looked him in the eye and said, 'I will not be a part of this slaughter.'

'You, William Weatherford,' Peter McQueen slowly began, his eyes cold and hard, 'go, go. Live like a white man that you are. Go now before I place my club between your eyes.'

'I beg of you, spare the lives of the women and the children,' William said slowly, looking at the Red Stick warrior. 'They have done nothing to you.' William Weatherford then turned and walked away, a great sadness filling his heart.

As he walked away, McQueen called out, 'Weatherford, we

knew that you would not be loyal to us.' Smirking, he continued, 'Weatherford, we have your family.'

"Suddenly, with fear covering his face, Billy and me began to walk in the direction of home of Bill's half brother, David Tate. Bill hoped that David could help find his family."

The Red Stick warriors returned to the Mims compound, their war clubs waving in the air and the sound of their blood-chilling war whoops announcing their return. The remaining Mims inhabitants had gathered up weapons and munitions fully expecting the return of the Red Sticks. Some men and women and their children hoped for refuge in an interior building which instead would be a death trap.

The second attack on the Mims fort was even more horrifying than the first had been. The following two or three hours were one of death and carnage. All but one or two of the inside structures had been set on fire by the Red Stick warriors. Most of the Tensaw people who had sought shelter and protection at the Mims compound would not live to return to their now burned farms. Thirty-five or forty fortunate ones had survived by fleeing the burning fortress and hiding in the woods. The remainder of their lives forever scarred for what would be remembered as the Fort Mims Massacre.

Chapter 16
Return to Talisi

"Word quickly spread on the frontier of what had happened at the Mims compound. Vultures circling in the air foretold of what had happened to the unfortunate ones inside. I, of course, left with Bill and this is what I was told later," Blue Sky man continued. "When the last victims no longer lived, the Red Stick warriors gathered up those fortunate or unfortunate to be take as captives and departed from the smoldering rubble that had been Fort Mims and camped a short distance away to recoup and count their dead. The Red Stick leaders were saddened and astonished when it was revealed that almost half of their number had perished in the battle."

Peter looked around the group of tired and wounded warriors, realizing that many of his friends were no longer accounted for. He looked over at Paddy Welch, who was nursing the wound that he had received. 'Paddy Welch,' Peter said in a cold voice, 'Paddy Welch, you are a fraud. You promised that the Great Spirit would protect our warriors from the bullets of the white man. Look around you. Your promise means nothing. Many, many of our brave warriors did not live to see the sunset of this day.' Peter paused, 'and for this, you too will not see the sunset.' The warriors at Peter's side instantly fired their muskets at Paddy Welch. Paddy fell to the ground at Peter's feet. 'Take him back to your Alabama Town. Do what you wish with him,' Peter said to several warriors who ran to Paddy's side.

When the sun was at its mid-point the following day, Peter and the Red Stick warriors began their journey back to their towns on the Tallapoosa and Coosa Rivers. Horses and cattle along with any other items of value that had not been burned had been taken from the Mims compound. The Red Sticks continued to raid and burn any plantation or farmstead they passed by, again taking what they pleased.

The occupants having long since fled in search of a place of refuge. The weary, frightened captives moved slowly, and the horses and cattle continued to stray from the path. This along with the plunder taken, made travel slow and eight suns had passed before the warriors returned to their upper town homes.

Peter and his Red Stick warriors were jubilant in their supposed victory but upset over the loss of several hundred warriors. Plans were already underway for more attacks on other outpost settlements and Peter knew the warriors would be missed. The Talisi warriors were welcomed home with great excitement and enthusiasm, the women and children running to greet them. This quickly changed when it became apparent to them that many of their husbands or love ones had not returned. They had not known of the loss the Red Stick warriors had suffered.

Elizabeth, the wife of Peter, ran to her husband with tears in her eyes. He held her briefly before pushing her away. 'I will talk to my people now,' he said softly. Peter looked over the large group of Talisi people who stood expectantly waiting for him, as their leader to speak. 'My people, my warriors have been victorious. Eight suns ago, the place called Mims was destroyed. Other than the few captives you see here and the few who escaped, no one there lives. We have killed the white men and Métis who were responsible for the death of warriors at Burnt Corn.' The Talisi people yelled out in response, then an old man, his hair gray and his face wrinkled with age called out to Peter.

'My Chief, where are the other warriors of our town? Their wives wait for them.'

'My father,' Peter began, 'the battle was big. Many white people, many Métis and,' he paused, many soldiers where at Mims. They had many guns and they fought well.' Not having to say more, the sound of loud keening filled the air. Women began tearing their clothing and scratching their arms.

'What of the words of the prophets who promised that the warriors would suffer no harm,' the man asked, tears running down his old face. 'My son,' he said, looking around, 'I do not see my son among the warriors that have returned.'

'My father, my people,' Peter said softly. 'The loss of our brave warriors will be avenged. The white man will not continue to take the homes or lives of our people.'

The triumph of victory had quickly turned into a time of sadness for the returning warriors and the Talisi people as well as the other towns the Red Stick warriors called home. Peter knew that to stop now, the loss of his warriors would have been in vain."

Chapter Seventeen
After Mims

"News of the massacre at Fort Mims, as it was soon called, spread rapidly. And just as soon, William Weatherford had been declared the half-breed devil that had led the Red Sticks. He was responsible for the horrific death of hundreds of men, women and even children. 'This will not be tolerated the officials and settlers of the Mississippi Territory had cried out. These savage people will be driven from this country. We will see to that.' In the meantime, these same settlers had sleeked refuge in Mobile and prayed that their homes would not be torched, and that they did not suffer the same fate as the people at Fort Mims.

William, after leaving the Mims battle site, had joined his half-brother, David Tate at Fort Pierce, three miles away from Mims. Tate, well-educated and prosperous, refused to declare allegiance to either the Red Sticks or the friendly Creek. He had left his wife Mary and her parents at Fort Mims, thinking they would be safe there. At the time he met with his brother, he did not know that she had perished. The half-brothers shared a warm relationship, and each was concerned about the other.

'William,' David anxiously asked, 'were you at Mims? What is the situation there? We heard gunfire. Mary and her ma and pa are there. Are they alright?'

'David, I do not know. There's been a battle. I pleaded with Peter and Josiah not to kill the women and children.' William dropped his head. 'I left when the warriors dropped back. Davey, many were killed on both sides. I cannot be a part of this. If I had it to do over, I would never have gone to Mims. Peter said my family would be killed if I did not.'

'William, I too wish you had not been a part of this,' David said softly, his voice breaking. 'I fear for my wife and the others. Oh, Bill, for God's sake, why did you side with them? You knew what the Red Sticks were capable of doing. Now you will be considered one of them.' The brothers clasped hands in the way of the Creek and William left to go in search of his family. David soon saw the billowing smoke on the horizon and the sorrowful word soon reached him that most were lost with only few surviving.

On the return trip, the Red Sticks did as Peter McQueen had said, and the settlers feared, burning and looting many of the farmsteads in the southwestern parts of the territory. Bill had found his family unharmed and returned home, refusing to be a part of the killing and destruction any more.

****

The hot summer turned into the cooler days of autumn and the time of turmoil and grief did not stop. The Red Sticks, still under the leadership of Peter McQueen, continued their rampage of the white settlers. Word had spread of the uprising against the white settlers and when help was asked for it was soon to come. The tide had turned, and militia arrived with the goal now to destroy the strong-hole towns and villages of the Red Sticks. By the time the white frost covered the ground battles had occurred at sites inside Indian territory. Crops had not been planted and there was no food and the women and children of the Red Sticks were hungry. They were now in danger. The soldiers came, just as the Red Stick warriors had gone to the white settlements. They came to the Creek town called Tallahatchee, killing the warriors and taking their women and children as prisoners. 'Retaliation,' they had said, 'for Fort Mims.'

Then the Red Stick warriors and the friendly Creeks began to fight among themselves. Hostile warriors attacked the village of Talladega for no reason except that they were friendly to the whites. One of the chiefs pulled a hog skin over his body and sneaked away from the attackers in search of help from troops from Tennessee. Four-hundred Red Stick warriors would fight no more. In each battle that took place their numbers became less, but they persisted in the quest to save their homelands from the white man.

Soon after the Talladega siege, a group of Tennessee volunteers attacked Hillabee Town on the Tallapoosa River. The Hillabee people had asked for peace and had no intention of fighting the whites. Warriors, their women and children were shot down as they came out of their houses to greet the soldiers. Many, many were killed. The betrayed survivors vowed now to fight alongside the Red Stick warriors.

The battles moved further down the Tallapoosa to Autossee where again warriors were surprised by militia from Georgia and friendly Creeks from a nearby town of Tuckabatchee. Two-hundred Red Stick warriors were slain, and the town was torched. The Creek people now lived in fear."

Blue Sky Man pushed his glass back and slowly rose from his chair. "Well," he said. "I am tired. If you care to hear the rest of my story about Billy and Peter, then meet me right here 'bout the middle of the morning tomorrow. There's plenty more to tell." He picked up his hat and slowly walked out the door into the dusty street.

James, the store owner, followed him watching in amazement and yelling out to him, 'Sir I will be right hear at 10AM sharp.'

Chapter Eighteen
Holy Ground

The following morning, Blue Sky Man met James inside the old general store. Two or three other old fellows had gathered around, all pulling up cane back chairs. Blue Sky's old wrinkled face lit up in a big smile when he realized he would have a bigger audience. "Well, morning to you all. Do y'all want to hear about Billy and Peter?" He asked. The old men nodded as James had filled them in from the notes he had taken. "Well, I tell you right now, most folks wouldn't believe me, but them two got a bad rap, especially Billy." He noticed that one of the old men wore a Confederate coat and another's arm hung limply at his side. "You two did some fight'n?" Both nodded again. "What was you fight'n for?"

'Why, we were fight'n for our homes and our land,' one said.

'All we wanted was to be left alone to live our life,' the other man said, vivid memories still alive in his eyes.

"Well, there you have it. That's all Billy and Peter and their people wanted too." Blue Sky man sat down, scratching his head. "Now, where was I? Oh, yeah, Ikana-Chaka, the Holy Ground."

****

"For weeks warriors had been moving their families over to the Alabama River town of Hossa-Yohola, prophet Josiah Francis. He had again declared the town to be a safe haven from the white militia. He had gone so far as to say that the Holy Ground would be a grave for the white man. William Weatherford too had taken his family there. He realized that the situation had escalated, and he feared for all of his Creek people. He still did not want to fight the white man, but he had no choice, his family and people came first.

Hundreds of Red Sticks and their families gathered at Holy Ground, which had become a fortress of sorts. Most of their weapons and supplies had been stored there. Josiah Francis had again promised the Creek people a place of refuge and safety. He did not know that a huge military contingent led by General Claiborne from Mississippi along with many other troops and volunteers and also warriors from the Choctaw were on their way.

Blue Sky Man leaned back in his chair and pulled his pipe from his shirt pocket and filled it with tobacco. After one of the old men offered a light, he settled back in his chair and began. "I remember just like it was yesterday."

'You were there,' James asked in awe?

"Course I was. I went everywhere with Billy back then. Might say I considered myself his bodyguard, not that he needed one," Blue Sky Man laughed. "It was a cold, cold day in December, the women and children were inside their houses. Me and Billy, along with some other warriors was sitting outside by the fire making plans, you know, just in case. Suddenly, some of the warriors who had been told to keep a lookout, started whooping and hollering and others closer to us started beating their drums. Boys, all heck broke loose then. One of the prophets started dancing round and round, waving a red cow's tail, trying to encourage the warriors. He soon lay dead on the ground. He had no more protection than anyone else.

The battle went on for only an hour or so, but many of the Red Stick warriors were killed. The women and children had been taken to safety and soon after that the warriors began to retreat too. Billy saw this and knew that all hope was over for the Red Sticks. He said for me to leave too, while I still could. I went down into a ravine where I was safe from the bullets and arrows that continued to fly. So, you see, I was able to see what really happened that day.

Billy was last to leave. Guess this was fit'n since he was the one leading the battle. The soldiers had him backed up nearly to the river with a stand of bushes between him and them. Billy knew right away what he had to do. He jumped on his big black horse; Arrow was his name. He rode back a ways as to give him a head start and swiftly rode toward the ravine," Blue Sky Man smiled. "Why he jumped right into the Alabama River. Spec it was about fifteen or twenty feet down from the bluff top. Both he and Arrow went all the way under. All I could see was Billy's rifle sticking out of the water. The horse, and he was a smart one, took off swimming. Then the soldiers started shooting at Billy and I was real scared for him, cause them bullets was splashing in the water all around him. One of them, nipping Arrow's mane. But, of course, Billy got safely to the other side and defiantly rode away on Arrow. Only one white soldier was killed, but twenty-one Red Stick warriors, including a leading Shawnee prophet, would not live to fight another day. Twelve black men were also killed. I thought this was odd, since the Red Sticks do not allow black men to fight with them, but I guess they needed their help that day," Blue Sky Man paused again and smiled. "So, that's the way it really happened at the place called Holy Ground."

Chapter Nineteen
Ole Hickory

Blue Sky man stood briefly and stretched before continuing, noticing that others had joined the group, eager anticipation showing on their faces. "Well," he began, "Well, after the big leap into the river, Billy joined the other Red Stick warriors. They was all shook up and decided it best to gather up their families and return to their home villages and regroup. Billy found his family and noticed right away that his wife Raney did not look well. He rested up for a bit then he and her and their little son, William, left for their home on the Coosa River." Blue Sky Man paused, his head down for such a long time that his audience thought the old man had dozed off. Suddenly he looked up with tears in his blue eyes and began talking again. "Raney, she was such a pretty one and Billy, why he loved her so. She walked the path to the Great Spirit on the twenty fifth day of December, Christmas Day it was. Never knew what sickness she had, guess it was one from the white man though. Billy was sad for a long time, but he kept right on trying to guide his people, mainly telling them that they couldn't win this battle with the white man. He knew it wasn't over for them."

Blue Sky man cleared his throat and looked over at the man behind the counter, who had pulled up his stool and was listening intently. "Sir, you reckon you could spare a cup of coffee? I'm getting awful dry and I got more, much more to tell."

'Certainly, why I've got a cup for everybody, and it's on the house,' the man replied with a smile. 'This is the best story I've heard in a long time, and it's true too!'

After the audience of six or eight mostly old men had cups of hot coffee in hand, Blue Sky man resumed his story, a faraway look in his eyes. "Sure, you all heard of old Andy Jackson." The men nodded and Blue Sky Man continued. "The man had a streak of meanness in him like a angry rattlesnake. He hated the Creeks and all Indians, fer that matter. Think I heard that his Paw and brother was killed by some Indians when he was just a boy. But I got to say, that he did have some good in him. He saved a little Creek boy from sure death in one of the battles. Took him home with him, he did, and he and his wife raised him like their own. Little fellow didn't live too long. Caught a white man's sickness and walked the path. And Ole Hickory as he was called, took a liking to Billy Weatherford. I'll tell you about that a little later on, getting ahead of myself, I am. Now, when it comes to the battles, he was all business. Meant to kill them all, he did, if he could."

"Course, by the time they got down here from up in Tennessee, hundreds of Red Sticks had already been killed and their numbers were decreasing quickly. Them white folks was serious too. They wanted the land of the Creeks. Had a mind to grow some cotton, they did, and them Creeks, why they didn't live like them white folks did anyway. Some folks called them just plain savages." Blue Sky Man shook his head, "I'm here to tell you right now, that ain't true. No offense, but I had heap rather had lived with my Creek family than my real relatives."

"But back to Ole Hickory. He and his Tennessee Volunteers came down here to Alabama like a bunch of stirred-up hornets. Thought they was gonna just run the Red Sticks out of here real easy like. But, no sir, it weren't like that at all. Put up a good fight, they did. Now you know I stayed with my friend Billy and he weren't involved in all these battles, in fact, he was only at two, Mims and the Holy Ground. There was another one in the fall of thirteen where he and Josiah Francis had some strong words and Billy and me, we just left. If I remember correctly," he laughed, "and I know I do, I was told that the Red Sticks gave old Hickory a good fight at a Creek called Emuckfau in January of fourteen and later that month at another village on the Tallapoosa."

"By then, the Red Sticks realized for themselves that this war was not going to be won by them. In desperation they planned for one more final showdown, but thinking back about it now, it may have been a place of defense. The place was on the upper Tallapoosa River and it was called Tohopeka or the Horseshoe. One-thousand Red Stick warriors and their families from the Hillabee, Oakfuskee, New Yauka, Eufaula and the Fish Pond towns came to what was a fortified village."

'Why was it called Horseshoe?' A younger man asked.

"You not from around here are you son?" Blue Sky Man asked, smiling.

'No sir,' the young man replied.

"Well, the Tallapoosa takes a big turn and forms an area of land in the shape of a horseshoe. Had the river on three sides, it did, with a small neck of land right in the middle. Well now, the Red Sticks knew them white soldiers and old Jackson was coming. They built," Blue Sky Man stopped and smiled again, "and I do admit that I helped them a bit before me and Billy left, a double fence made of trees so strong a mean old bull couldn't break through. Why, it was higher than a man stands tall and had holes to shoot out of. I ain't never seen a white man build anything so strong."

'Why did you and Weatherford leave? And, you have not mentioned Peter McQueen. Was he there at the Horseshoe battle?' The same young man asked.

"Well now, glad you asked," Blue Sky Man answered. "Billy had received word that he was needed back home. Something about family business. I think he wouldn't have left if he had known when the fight was going to be. And Peter, he was not there either. He spent most of his time dealing with them white folks on the other side of the Creek Nation, near the Chattahoochee River. He told me later on," Blue Sky Man laughed, "that if he had been there, things might have been different." Blue Sky Man paused again, "I don't think it would have mattered. It would have been the same."

Blue Sky Man stood and stretched his long arms and looked out at his audience, which now included several women. "If you all will excuse me for a few minutes, I need to walk outside and gather my thoughts."

'I'll fix us all some more coffee,' the storekeeper said.

'And I have a basket of freshly baked cookies here. I think there is plenty for everyone.'

Blue Sky Man came back inside and settled back down in the wicker back chair. Without any introduction he began, his voice trembling. "It was Sunday, the twenty-seventh day of March 1814. A cold day for that late in the spring. Scouts had been sent out and the Red Sticks were ready. The women and children and men too old and feeble to fight had been crowded into the hastily prepared town beside the river for protection. Ole Jackson led his troops and volunteers, and there were over two-thousand strong, down the Tallapoosa. He had looked in amazement at the breastwork the Red Stick warriors had built but realized immediately they would be slaughtered. He also had been told by his scouts that the families of the Red Sticks were behind them down near the river. He ordered his trusted friend, General Coffee, was his name, to circle back and cross the river to prevent the Red Sticks form escaping."

Blue Sky Man paused again and swallowed hard. "The sun was well up in the sky, I guess about ten o'clock. Jackson from his position, high on a hill, started firing his two cannons down on the Red Sticks. The cannon balls came close, but just missed the barricade. I, remember, was not there. I was told the prophets started their dancing and singing." Blue Sky Man shook his head. "Poor fools. This carrying on could not save nobody from what was to happen. Well, the cannon firing went on for a while, then Jackson, he noticed smoke down by the river. It seemed that Coffee had crossed back to the other side and had stormed the village. Two or three canoes had been left on the riverbank for escape, just as Jackson had thought. Some Cherokee and friendly Creeks swam the cold river and took the canoes back to the soldiers. Ole Jackson, he was mean man, but he was smart. He knew the Red Stick warriors would go back to their families when they saw the smoke. So, he charged his soldiers down the hill and then the fighting really began. Didn't take long before them soldiers were climbing the log barricade and getting inside." Tears begin trickling down the old man's face. "The slaughter continued for a long time. Then it was over. When the sun set near one-thousand Red Stick warriors lay in heaps on the ground. Only a few survived to tell what really happened that day. The massacre of Fort Mims had now been avenged, the white people said."

The small group of people sat in silence with visions of the horror they had just heard. The same inquisitive young man who had asked questions earlier, quietly said, 'one-thousand warriors slain. Do you know how many actually survived?'

"As I said, some did, of course," Blue Sky Man answered. "Many were hurt really bad and walked the path later. Some tried to escape by jumping into the river." He shook his head. "Most didn't make it either. Well, I do know one who did." He smiled, "Old Menawa."

'Menawa, who was he?' Another man asked.

"Why, Menawa, he was the Red Stick leader at the Horseshoe. Menawa took Monahee's place when he went down with a musket ball in the mouth. You see, he was one of the prophets that thought he could not be killed. Menawa was shot many times but managed to hide under some of the dead warriors until the soldiers left the battlefield. He then floated down the river to safety. A brave man he was. Determined to live. I was told later on that Billy was supposed to lead the Red Sticks, but he did not agree with the prophets and that was the real reason we left, not because of business at home."

The old woman who had shared the cookies, tearfully asked, 'the women and children, what happened to them?'

"They were taken prisoner," Blue Sky Man said. "Some of them were taken down river to Tuckabatchee Town, some over to the Chattahoochee River and the Cherokee took some back to their towns. The women, they were strong and the Spirit of the Creek grandmothers helped them along the way."

The sun was high in the sky when Blue Sky Man finished telling about the battle at the Horseshoe. He was tired and his audience all said they had things to do, but surely would like to hear more.

The storekeeper scratched his head and smiled, 'how 'bout meeting down at the Baptist Church later this afternoon. I'm a deacon and I'm sure the preacher won't mind. Shoot, he will most likely come too.'

Blue Sky Man turned to see that the room was nearly full of people, all who said they would come to listen later. 'I'll go home and bake more cookies," the Cookie Lady said.

'I've got fresh bread I'll bring,' another added.

'Coffee's on me,' the storekeeper said cheerfully. 'See you all at three o'clock. I want to know what happened to Billy and learn more about this Peter McQueen.'

Chapter Twenty
Broken Spirit

Later that afternoon, Blue Sky Man ambled down the road to the small white clabber board church. He was amazed when he saw the church was packed with people. The storekeeper waved when he came in the door.

'Hello there,' the man said cheerfully. 'We were afraid you had forgotten.'

"No sir," Blue Sky Man answered. "I could never forget this story. I just," pausing as he looked over the large group of people. "I am surprised and honored to see so many."

'We want to hear your story Blue Sky Man,' the young man who had asked so many questions earlier said. 'And, we are ready for you to begin.'

'Come on up here and make yourself comfortable,' the storekeeper said.

"Been in some churches before, but never stood or sat where a preacher did,' Blue Sky Man declared. "Let's see now, where did I leave off?"

'The slaughter at the Horseshoe and the women and children were taken captive,' the cookie lady yelled out.

Blue Sky Man sighed, "Oh yes. Well, with nearly all the Red Stick warriors gone, the Creek War as it was called, was almost over. The few remaining survivors from the Horseshoe went back to their villages, those that the white man had not destroyed, anyway. Some of them, fortunately had not brought their families with them. Still fearing that ole Jackson's soldiers would follow them, the warriors took their families and gathered together to hide deep in the woods. Others took off for Spanish Florida. You see, the Battle at the Horseshoe had broken the Spirit of the Creek people. Oh, there would still be little raids on some of the white farms and some of the Red Stick leaders still claimed that they would rise again. But it was over."

'What happened to the leader Me-Menawa?' Someone asked.

"Menawa wore the scars of the battle for the rest of his life, but he lived and continued to lead his people. This might surprise you, but Menawa actually helped the white soldiers years later when there was another short war. That was just before the Creeks were made to leave their homes. He agreed to help bring in the small remainder of Red Stick warriors that caused problems for the growing number of white settlements. For his help, after having been told that he could stay in his home, he was forced to join his people. The strong, valiant Menawa walked the path of the Great Spirit and was buried in an unmarked grave on the Trail Where They Cried.

'And Billy Weatherford and McQueen what happened to them,' still another inquired?

"When Billy heard what had happened at the Horseshoe, he took all of his people and many others joined him and they hid too. He knew then, they would come after him. Peter still considered to be one of the most important and feared Red Stick leaders got his family together and took off to Florida. One of his family members, ten-year-old Billy Powell and his mother Polly, made the trip with them. Some of you may have heard of Billy when he became a man, he was known as Osceola."

Many in the crowded room gasped at the name and once again the inquisitive young man called out to Blue Sky Man, 'Osceola?'

"Yes sir he was," Blue Sky Man answered. "Now I could be wrong 'bout this, but I believe little Billy Powell was Peter's nephew. Most of the families were connected one way or another either by their red blood or their white blood. But off to Florida they went. Some of them never came back up here to Alabama."

'What about Peter, did he come back?' And old man from the back of the room yelled out.

"No, no not to live," Blue Sky Man replied. "As a Red Stick warrior, Peter, all his life, both in Alabama and Florida, looked for and found trouble. He continued raiding and causing problems for the white settlers. Caused so much trouble, he did, that the government sent troops out to look for him, wanted to hang him I 'pect. I heard that my old friend Peter spent the last year or two of his life wondering around south Florida and on some of them little islands just off the coast. Folks never saw him again or heard from him," Blue Sky Man paused, a sad look covering his wrinkled face. Guess he got sick or injured some way and walked the path to the Great Spirit. Billy, he was real sad about never seeing him again. Said he deserved better. That he loved his homeland and did not think the white folks had any right to take it from his people."

Chapter Twenty-One
Save My People

"Back to Bill Weatherford; Billy, he never did understand why the soldiers and the white people thought he was so important and the leader of all the Creek Indians. Shoot, he could have passed for a white man if he had wanted to. I told y'all he weren't even at most of the battles. All he wanted to do was help his mother's people. He was smart and knew what was going to happen," Blue Sky Man remarked.

'So, what did happen to Billy and his people when they hid in the woods,' the storekeeper asked? 'And did Ole Jackson go looking for them after the Horseshoe?'

"Well, after the terrible battle, some of Jackson's volunteer troops went back up to Tennessee, you know their time was up," Blue Sky Man laughed. "Fact was, their time had been up for a good while, but Ole Jackson, he threatened to shoot them if they left afore he was through with them. That was the kind of man he was. Mean and hard, even to his own. But after he rested up for a few days after the battle, he took off down the river for that French fort down where the Tallapoosa and Coosa Rivers run together to make the Alabama. He had his men go to building a new fort. Wanted one named after him, he thought a lot of himself, you know. Course the soldiers searched for any Creeks that might be wandering around. Now, that brings us back to Billy. He had taken all of his people he could round up, took'em deep in the woods, a long way from any paths the soldiers knew about. They were a pitiful bunch, they were."

Blue Sky Man paused, tears forming again in his eyes. "Weren't no food to speak of, they had to live off what the woods and little streams provided. Only clothes they had were on their backs. Some of them did have tattered blankets. In desperation, waving white flags, some had already turned themselves in to the soldiers at Jackson's camp."

"Me and Billy tried to round all the others up. I can still hear them babies ah crying and the old ones moaning. Billy knew he had to do something to help," Blue Sky Man said sadly. "Billy, with tears in his eyes, turned to me and said." 'Blue Sky Man, I have no choice. I cannot allow my people to suffer in this way. I know that Jackson wants me and if I turn myself in to him, surely he will help them and allow them to live.'

Blue Sky Man paused, the faraway look again covering his wrinkled face, "but Billy, he will hang you if you go to him, I said. Billy replied to me in a strong voice," 'If that is my fate Blue Sky, then so be it.'

"The next morning, Billy contacted Sam Manac, his brother-in-law and told him his plans. Manac then got the word to Ole Jackson himself and told him Billy was coming. Billy, he wouldn't let me go with him, said I was a white man, and this was not my battle. Said he loved me like a brother. I put up a fuss, but Billy still said no. What I tell you now was told to me by another friend of Billy. He was going to take Billy to the camp of Jackson and help him understand his words. You remember, I told you that Billy, as smart as he was, sometimes did not understand the fancy words of the white man."

"With heavy heart, I watched as Billy, his clothing soiled and tattered, mounted on a borrowed horse. He turned and looked at me one final time, before he turned to ride, not knowing what was ahead for him. Friends, I tell you I have never knowed any man that showed such strength and courage as Billy did," Blue Sky lamented.

Chapter Twenty-Two
Ole Jackson, Face to Face

"Again, this is what was told to me. The soldiers starred in disbelief when Billy and his friend rode into Fort Jackson. One or two of them had recognized him. Billy's friend did the talking and asked for General Jackson. Ole Jackson came out of his tent, his clothing wrinkled, and his red hair ruffled. The General and the Creek warrior looked intently at each other. Billy, he spoke first and asked him if he was General Jackson. The man answered that he was. I was told that Billy stood up straight and said, 'I am Bill Weatherford.' Jackson nodded and asked him, his voice cold as ice, why he had come to his camp."

"Billy, he said, 'General Jackson, I have come to turn myself in to you. I cannot continue to fight you and the white soldiers. Most of my warriors lie dead on the battlefields and they can fight no more. I will tell you the truth, sir, that if I had warriors who could fight, I would never surrender.'

"Ole Jackson, he continued to look hard into the eyes of Billy and Billy, I was told, never flinched a muscle," Blue Sky Man said proudly. "Billy, speaking softly said, my people, the women and children and old men are hidden deep in the woods. I will bring them in to you,' he paused, 'if you will give them food and shelter. If you refuse, they will die.'

"Ole Jackson nodded and said, 'Weatherford, I will allow you to go get your people. I will do as you asked, but,' he paused. 'But if you do not return or if you raise a hand in battle against any of my soldiers, you will die. I will see to it personally.'

Blue Sky Man cleared his throat and then continued, "there were several old chiefs in camp. They were friendly with the white folks, you know. Well, they all started hollering and carrying on so, you would have thought a pack of devils was after them. 'Kill him, kill him, they yelled out."

"Well, Ole Jackson, he turned to them, holding up his hand

and said, 'any man with the courage to come into this hostile camp and surrender deserves to live.' Blue Sky Man smiled, "Ole Jackson, he turned back to Billy. 'Come with me, I imagine you are hungry. So, they both went inside Jackson's tent. A meal was provided for Billy along with a glass," Blue Sky Man smiled again. "Several glasses of bourbon. Why, the two men, who earlier had been hated enemies, after talking awhile, became almost friendly. Both recognized the strength of the other."

"After he got his people into Fort Jackson, Billy then left, and with me by his side, and slipped back to his farm in the southern part of the State. He quickly realized this was a mistake. It seems many of his enemies both white and red where waiting for him. Billy figured they were there to kill him, so we went on over to Fort Claiborne. Ole Jackson, on hearing that his newfound friend, was in danger, had him removed to a place where he would be safe. I was allowed to go."

Blue Sky Man, laughing out loud began talking again, "before it was all over with, Ole Jackson provided Billy with a fine horse and had him taken up to Tennessee to his big house. He hid himself out up there, stayed for a long while, he did. Ole Jackson knew that Billy would be killed if the white folks found him. So, that's the story of Billy Weatherford's surrender to Ole Andy Jackson."

Chapter Twenty-Three
White Doe

Blue Sky Man stood up, looking over all the folks who had crowded into the little church. "Think I need to stretch my legs and walk about for a bit. Getting a little hungry, I am. Be nice if we all could share some of that food and coffee over there." He proclaimed, smiling. "Smells mighty good. When I get back, I will finish up my story about Billy and there is more to tell about Peter too."

When Blue Sky Man returned, the women had covered a table in the corner with a clean, white cloth and filled the plates with freshly baked cookies and bread. Pots of hot coffee simmered on the pot belly stove in the back of the room. After the refreshments had been enjoyed, Blue Sky Man returned to the chair he had occupied earlier. He suddenly looked like the tired old man that he was. The faraway look had returned to his eyes. He cleared his throat and began talking, his voice noticeably weaker. "Afore I talk about my friend Billy, let me go back and tell you good folks a little bit more about that rascal Peter."

'Why do you call him a rascal sir?' The same inquisitive man asked.

Blue Sky Man laughed, "Well now, I reckon it's because he picked on me, called me a little white-skin boy, he did. Y'all remember now, that I told you I had lived with the Creek people all those years ago." Blue Sky Man paused, tears forming in his eyes as he remembered the past. "Spent a lot of time with Billy and Peter. Truth is, I was fond of him too. But him and Billy, they wuz different. Billy was calm and thought things out and Peter, well he was a hot head, just did things without thinking a' tall. Well, as I was about to say, Peter, he was one of the main Red Stick leaders, you know. And he will always be known for that. He was involved in lots of battles, killed many a white man, he did. All the fight'n and killing didn't change nothing. When it was all over, the white people won and took the land of the Creeks."

"Now, back to Billy. Remember I told y'all he stayed up in Tennessee at Ole Jackson's house for a long spell, maybe even a year. When the fight'n tween the Creeks and the whites was over, Billy went back to his home on the Tensaw River. Kept mighty quiet, he did. Folks still thought of him as the leader of the Red Sticks and the reason all them white people was killed. Now that I told you the story, you know that weren't the truth a tall. Fact was, he tried his best to prevent the fight'n. As more time went by, the feeling folks had for him changed some and he became respected and even liked."

Blue Sky Man laughed again and continued, "Why, I remember Billy and me went over to one of them places that serves up food and drinks for folks. While we wuz eating our supper, three old rough-looking fellows walked in and had them a few glasses of whisky. Well, they wuz talking among themselves and don't you know that sometimes when fellows get to drinking, they begin to do some mighty big talking." Blue Sky Man laughed again and continued, "Well, sir, one of them remarked with his whisky glass held up high," 'Like to meet this William Weatherford. I would tell that stinking red heathen a thing or two.'

"Couldn't help myself and I slowly pushed my chair back and walked over to the table. Sir, I said, politely, so you would like to meet Billy Weatherford? The fellow answered me, 'Well I, sure would.' I smiled broadly and pointed my hand to Billy and said, may I present to you Mr. William Weatherford." Blue Sky Man started laughing. Won't never forget the look on the old fellow's face. He and his buddies almost tripped over each other as they ran out the door."

"Well, Billy, he continued to do good with this farm, shoot, some folks even called it a plantation. He married again in 1817, she was a good woman. They got married in a white ceremony, they did. She and Billy had a nice family, believe they had four of five young'uns. She was sister to a Mr. Stiggins who later on wrote himself a book about Red Eagle." Blue Sky Man paused as his audience looked at him in confusion. "Oh, I forgot to tell you, but at some point, not real sure when, but folks, both red and white begin calling Billy, Red Eagle. That's the name he is called by today."

'Why,' the inquisitive young man asked.

"It was because of the loud yell he gave during battle. Sounded like the shrill cry of an eagle, it did," Blue Sky Man answered, smiling.

"Billy and Mary continued to do well and became quite wealthy with his plantation. Most of his neighbors thought well of him and then seemed to forget that he had been considered a Red Stick savage. Me and him still spent a lot of time together. I helped him some around the plantation, but we spent most of our time talking about the good and the bad of our past. Did a lot of hunting, we did. We really enjoyed that. Now, don't you know, that he was still a real good shot. Why, he could hit a dear fifty yards away. One day in early spring, but the weather was still cold, he said to me, 'Blue Sky, I got a hankering to kill me a bear. Let's me and you get a bunch of fellows together and go off down the river and do some bear hunting.'

"So, a few days later, we packed up and went down river. Went in some thick woods and put up a camp, we did. Had us a real good time. Billy, he killed him a big ole black bear," Blue Sky Man laughed. "Wish 'ah could have seen his face. Looked like a kid, he did. He was so proud. Well, it turned off real cold, so we started back upriver. Hadn't walked very far when we seen this big white doe. Now, you know, you don't see many white deer. Billy, he stopped and looked real close at the deer. He, like all Creek Indians was really superstitious," Blue Sky Man paused with that sad for away look again covering his face. "Billy, softly said," 'one of us will soon walk the path.' Blue Sky paused again and looked down this time for so long his audience thought he had dosed off. When he looked up, tears streaked his wrinkled old face. "Billy took sick when we got home. The doctor came but said weren't nothing he could do. March 9, 1824, Billy walked the path to the Great Spirit. Oh, Billy," Blue Sky Man said with the emotion of just seeing a loved one pass away. "Oh, Billy."

After sitting silently for a few minutes, Blue Sky Man looked out over his audience, tears still sparkling in his now dull blue eyes. "My friends, that is my story about one of the bravest, kindest men that I ever knowed. That is the story of Camouttee, the Truth-Maker, the Red Eagle. He was buried beside his mother, Princess Sehoy, not far from the river." Blue Sky Man slowly stood and began walking toward the church door and shuffled down the wooded steps.

'Wait, where are you going? Its cold out there and soon will be night,' one of the men called out.

Blue Sky Man turned and looked at the crowd of people who stood in the doorway. He smiled, "I must go now, my story has been told and my time here is finished. Remember me and remember my friend Peter and my brother Billy. Remember they were people just like you and all they really wanted was to be allowed to live their lives in their own ways in the homeland of their grandfathers."

The group of people who had just heard the story of William Weatherford, The Red Eagle, watched the old man slowly walk down the narrow road. Just as the sunset, a large white doe crossed his path.

****

Chapter Twenty-Four
The Journal

Matthew closed the old journal and looked up at Jacob, his voice breaking as he said, "My goodness, my goodness."

Jacob looked back at him, both young men almost speechless with emotion. "I, I feel like we have just taken a journey back to a different time and met the men who were a big part of our history."

"That is a good way to explain it Jacob. It's like we ourselves actually met Billy Weatherford and Peter McQueen. I've read and studied about these men, but nothing compares to this. Thanks to Aunt Minnie Raintree, we have this information."

"Yeah, and to Blue Sky Man too," Jacob added. "What a character he must have been, being friends with Peter and like a brother to Billy."

"And the experiences he had because of his friendship with them. What a wonderful story, a true story at that," Matthew said, opening the old tattered journal again. "Wait, what's this," He said as a small pamphlet, yellow with age fell from the journal. Matthew carefully picked up the fragile pamphlet. "Whoa, look at this. Its dated 1870 and the name on the front says *Tallassee Mills Briefs*."

"Oh man, what is this all about," Jacob asked excitedly.

"Listen to this. Tallassee, Alabama, October 1870. An unusual visit was made to our town last week by a man who said his name was Blue Sky Man. Nice old man he was. He dropped by the Mill Company Store, out of nowhere it seemed. He said he had a story to tell and he just began to talk. Two or three old fellows were in the store at the time, but before long the audience grew and along with coffee and fresh-baked cookies, all ended up at the Baptist Church. He began his story by telling how his kin had been murdered by white folks and he had been taken in and raised by some Creek Indians. He told of being friends with the Red Eagle and Peter McQueen. What a wonderful, fascinating, true story I might add. He told them about these Indian men and the fine time was had by all. Just as the sun began to set, he said his story was finished. He rose from his chair and slowly walked down the street. Several in the audience recalled seeing a white doe cross his path as he walked. No one has seen Mr. Blue Sky Man since. …

Jacob looked up and smiled, "I cannot believe this, this stroke of luck."

"Jacob," Matthew said softly. "This is not luck. It was meant to be. It all began with Aunt Minnie Raintree and the wonderful story she told of her family, Soaring Eagle, Little Flower and the others. This is not just a coincidence either. I mean you and," he paused, "me too, being Anthropology majors. I'm telling you Jacob, there's a reason for this. Do you think anyone has seen or will ever see the things we have seen, right here in this cotton field?" Matthew paused again, "Jacob, I don't understand this at all. And I know we would be accused of being a couple of crazy guys if we told what had happened here, but Jacob, it did happen. It scares me, but it happened!"

"I know, buddy. You are right," Jacob said, his voice shaking as he spoke.

Matthew paused, taking a deep breath, "You know what Jacob? I think this all started with our fishing trip down here on the river several years ago. You said yourself that you could feel the spirit of the Creek people who lived here long ago," Matthew said smiling as he remembered his friend experiencing what himself had felt all his life. "Let's try and get some sleep now," Matthew said, yawning, looking at his cellphone. "Man, it's already past midnight. He smiled, "Want to pull out Aunt Minnie Raintree's sleeping bags like we did the last night we were here?"

"Why not," Jacob said happily. Know what? This place is beginning to feel like home."

Both young men were soon sleeping soundly. Matthew heard the yelping of the coyotes first, then Jacob was awakened too. "Matthew sounds like the coyotes are just outside," Jacob whispered softly. "Do you think?"

"Only one way to find out buddy," Matthew said, sliding out of his sleeping bag.

Both quietly walked to the door and slipped out on to the small porch just in time to see a pack of five or six coyote racing in front them. Matthew caught his breath when he saw the glimmer of firelight suddenly appear out in the field and heard the soft sound of the drumbeat. "Jacob, I think it's happening," Matthew said, his heart racing.

"I know Matthew," Jacob replied. "I had hoped it would."

They watched as shadowy figures appeared before them, dancing slowly, then faster around the fire. They recognized a woman they had seen before as Little Flower and as the watched another older woman appeared. "Look, its Aunt Minnie Raintree," Matthew whispered.

Then warriors joined the dance, first Soaring Eagle and others they had not seen before. Firelight shinning on their painted faces, one holding his war club high over his head. The other paused, giving the shrill, piercing cry of an eagle. Both Matthew and Jacob knew instantly that the figures they were seeing where that of Peter McQueen and the Red Eagle. Then, a tall old man, obviously white, joined the others, his blue eyes flashing as he danced.

Both Matthew and Jacob stood in amazement and disbelief at what they were seeing. Just as the night sky began to turn gray, the drum slowed, and the group of figures all stopped and looked in the direction of the little cabin and the boys as if bidding them farewell and then they were gone.

In the years to come, Matthew and Jacob both would be successful in their fields of Anthropology. They along with their wives would spend much time at the old cabin. Their wives were never told why their husbands would suddenly leave the cabin in the middle of the night to go outside, and never understood why, on occasion, both Matthew and Jacob would come back inside with a glazed, faraway look in their eyes. They would hint of the strange, unexplained events, but never told of what they had witnessed in the old cotton field which had belonged to Aunt Minnie Raintree and her people.

The End

Epilogue

Historical events are amazing and often on their own make for an interesting story. But, on the other hand, facts sometimes do get confusing and bogged down and are often incorrect. I have done extensive research on the lives of William Weatherford and Peter McQueen, so I think I am accurate on their real-life details. This research combined with a fictitious character, Blue Sky Man, tells their story as a witness of the times. I hope this approach made the *The Cry of the Eagle* entertaining as well as a learning experience.

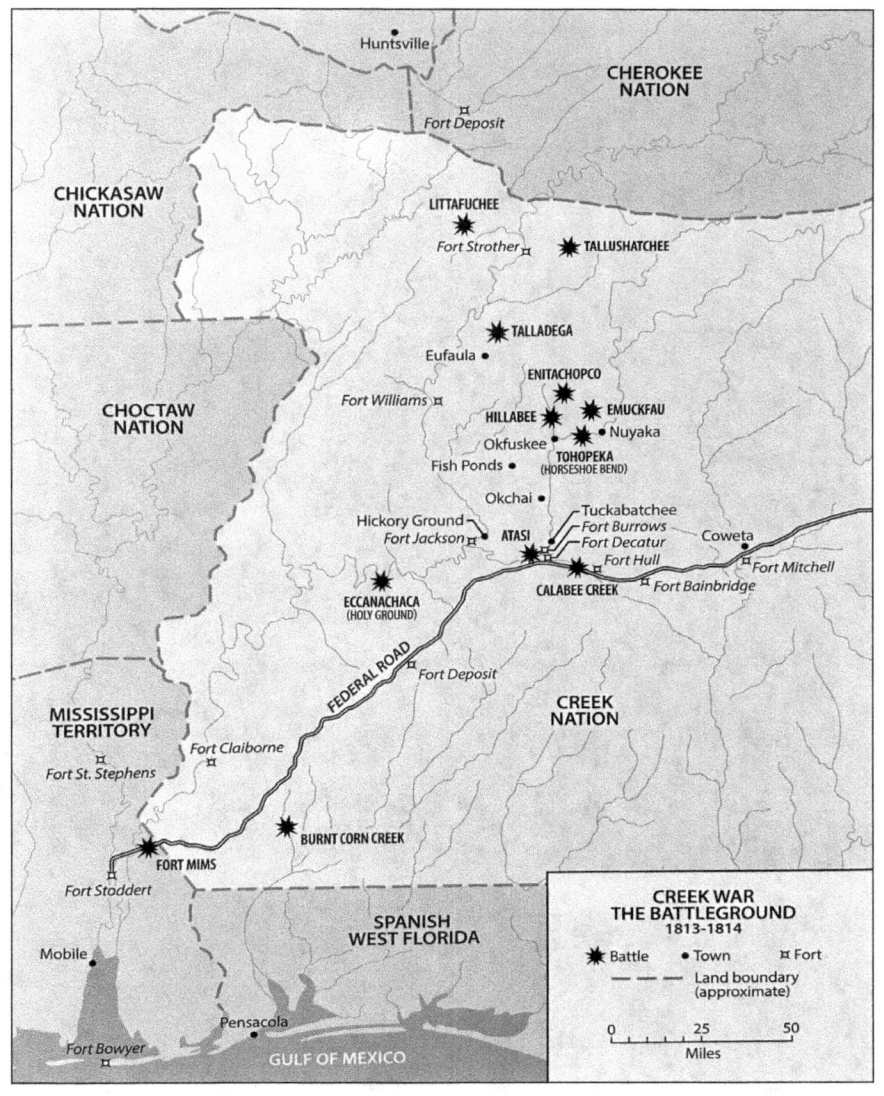

Debra Hughey

Burnt Corn

Burnt Springs Historic Marker

Large White Building at Burnt Corn

Abandoned Store Building at Burnt Corn

Another Old Store at Burnt Corn

Coca Cola 5 Cents at Burnt Corn General Store

FORT Mims

DAR Marker at Fort Mims

Engraved Stone Marker at Fort Mims

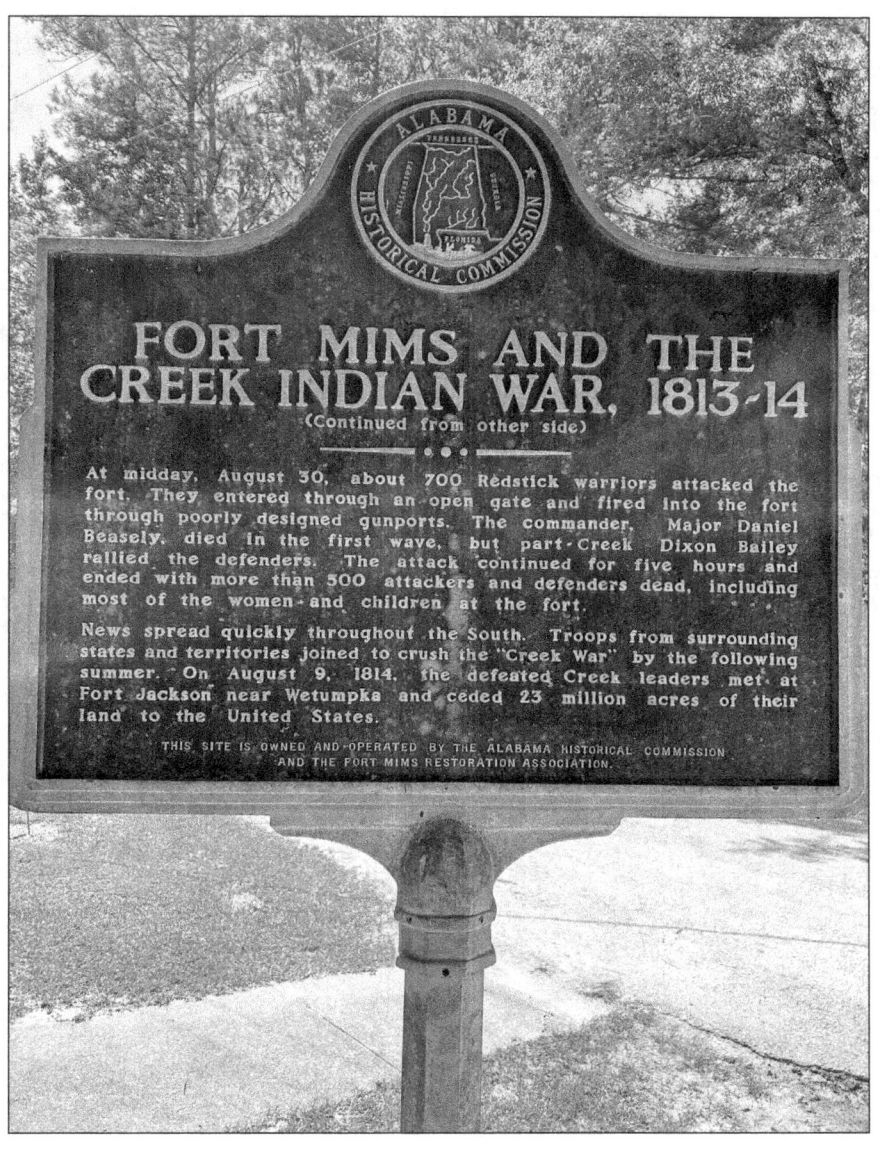

Ft. Mims Historic Marker

Reproduction of the Block House at Ft. Mims

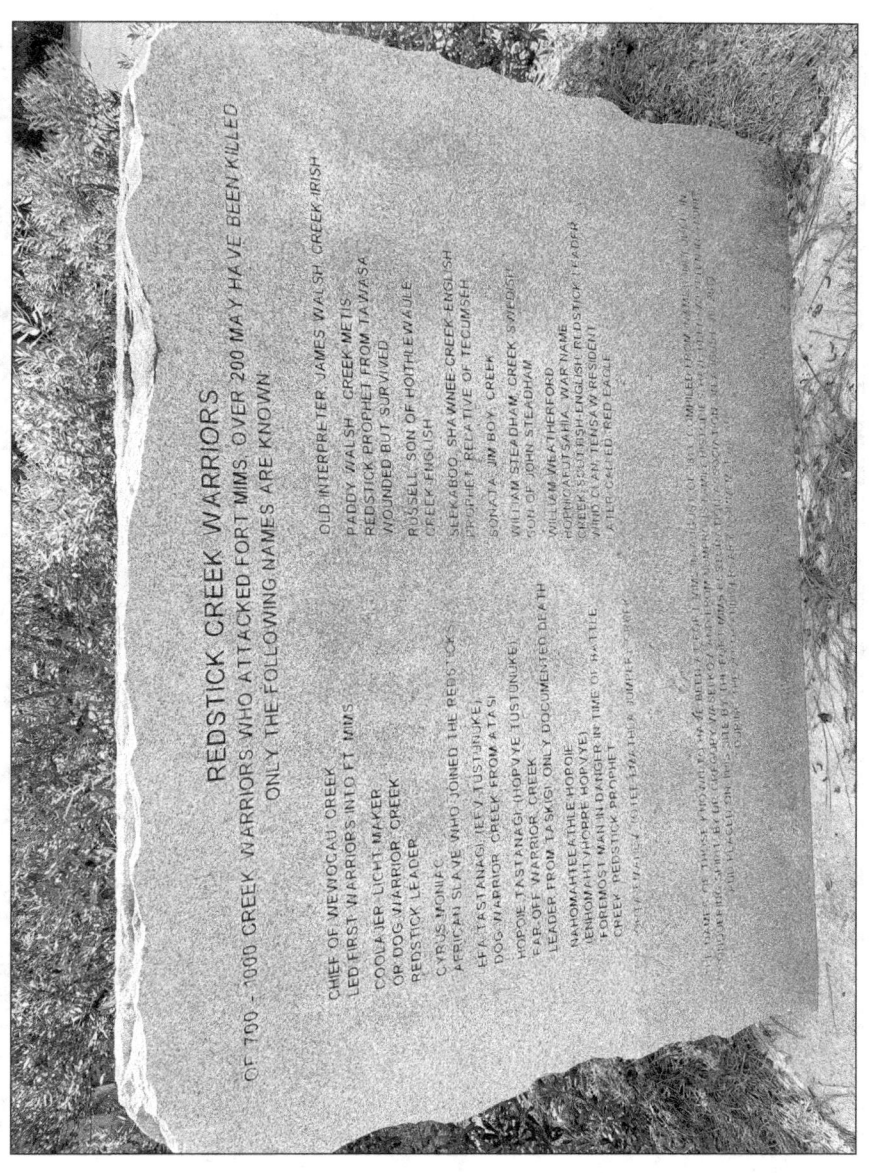

Red Sticks Who Fought at Fort Mims

Tensaw Residents Killed at Fort Mims — Marker No. 1

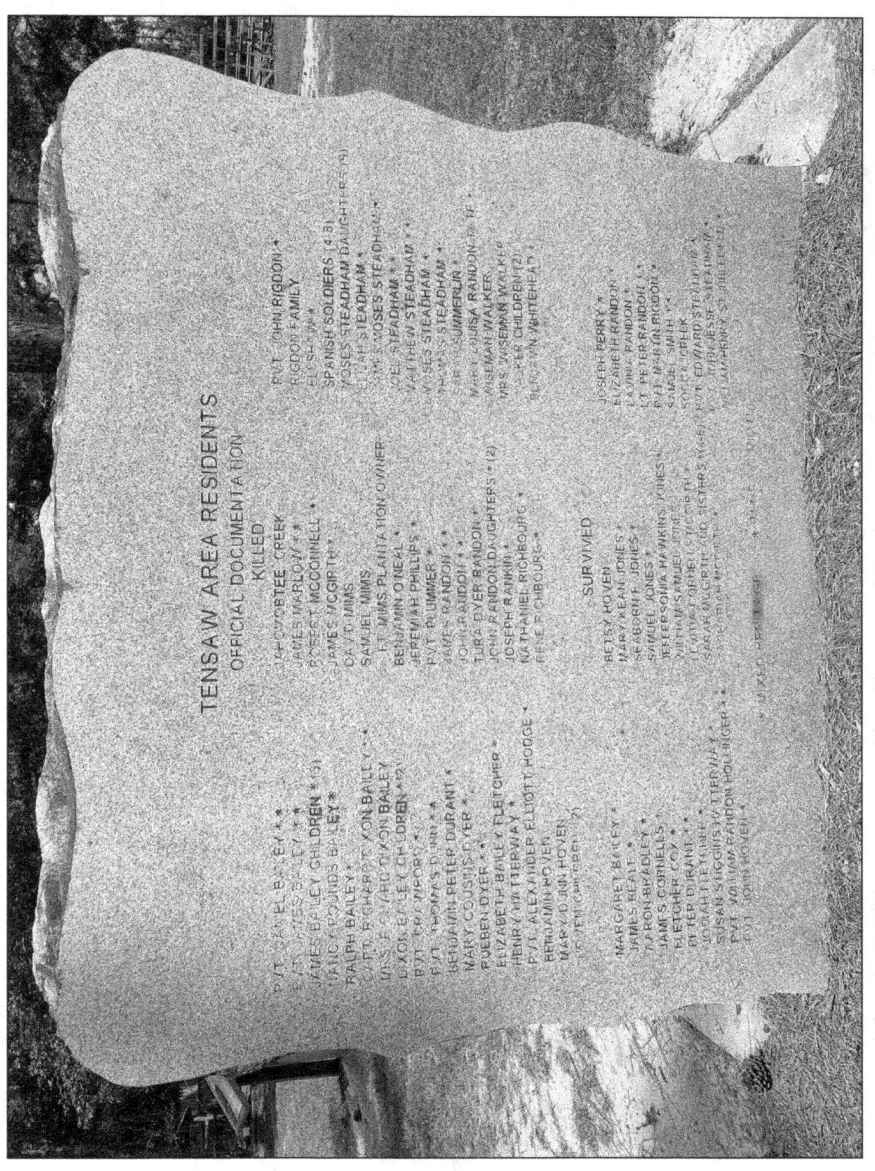

Tensaw residents killed No. 3 at Ft. Mims

Interior of Ft. Mims Blockhouse

Ft. Mims East Gate

Debra Hughey at Ft. Mims East Gate

Museum at Fort Mims

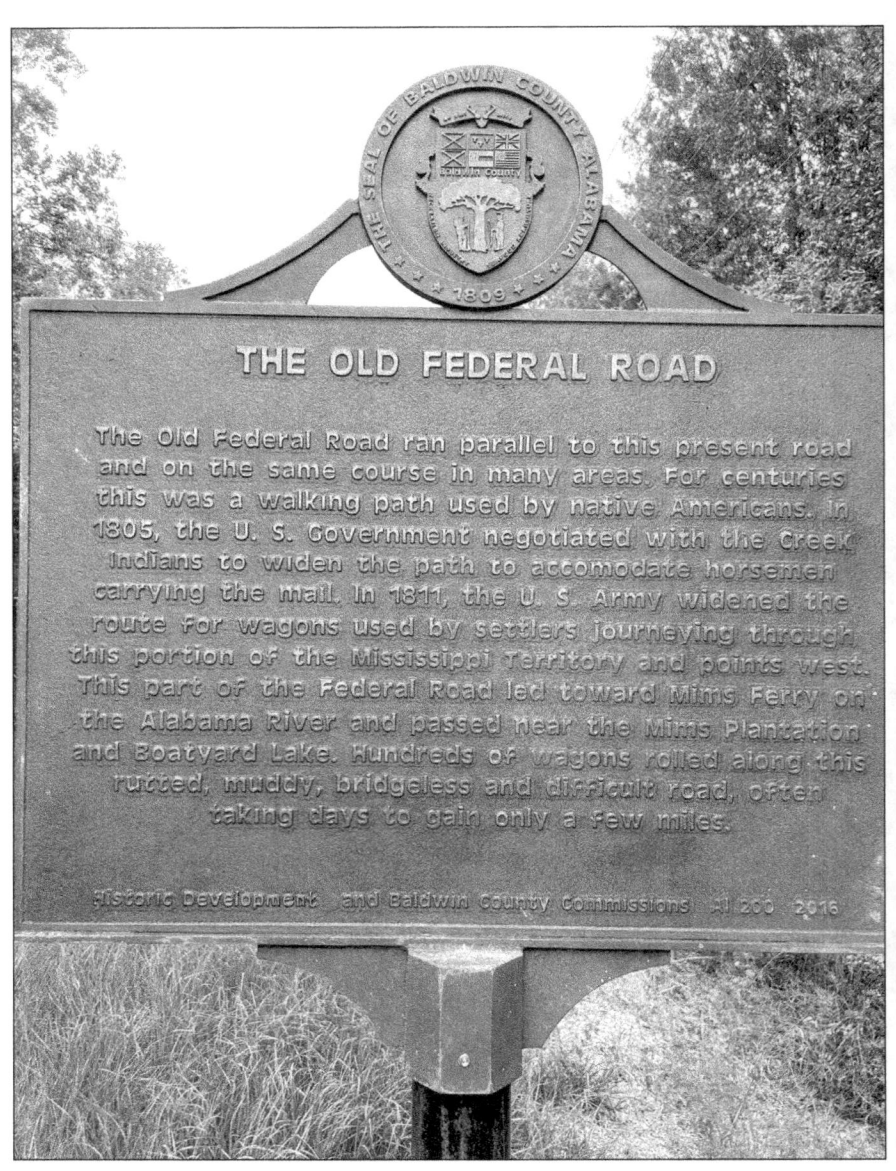

Old Federal Road Historic Marker near Fort Mims

Fort Mims Massacre Painting

William Weatherford Monument

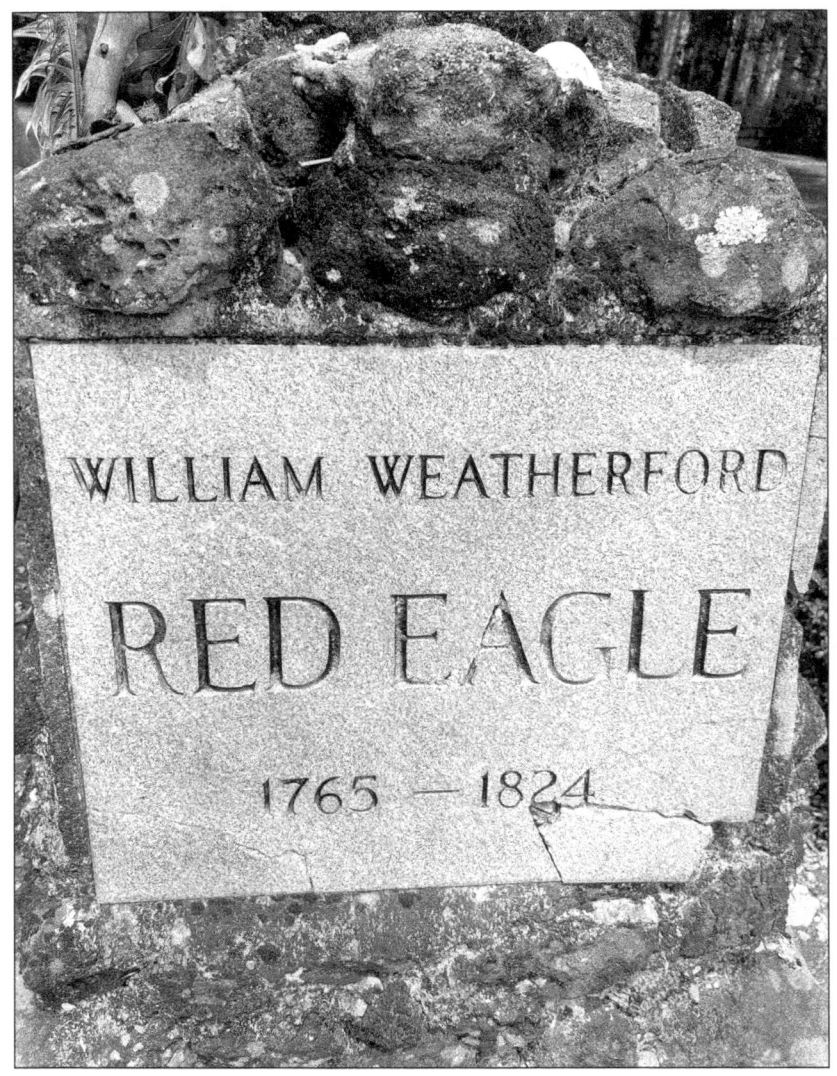

William Weatherford Grave Marker

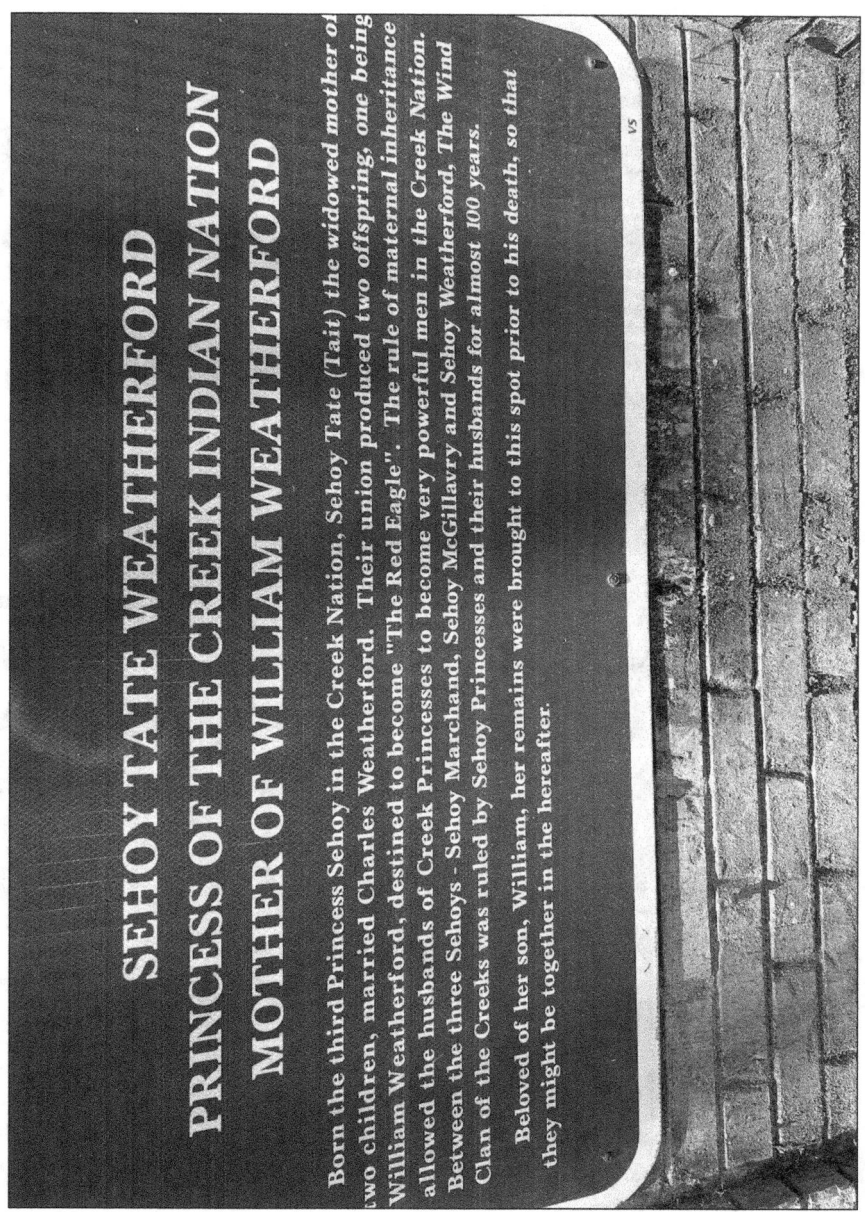

History of Red Eagle's Mother, Sehoy

William Weatherford Monument: Red Eagle's Mother, Sehoy Grave Stone

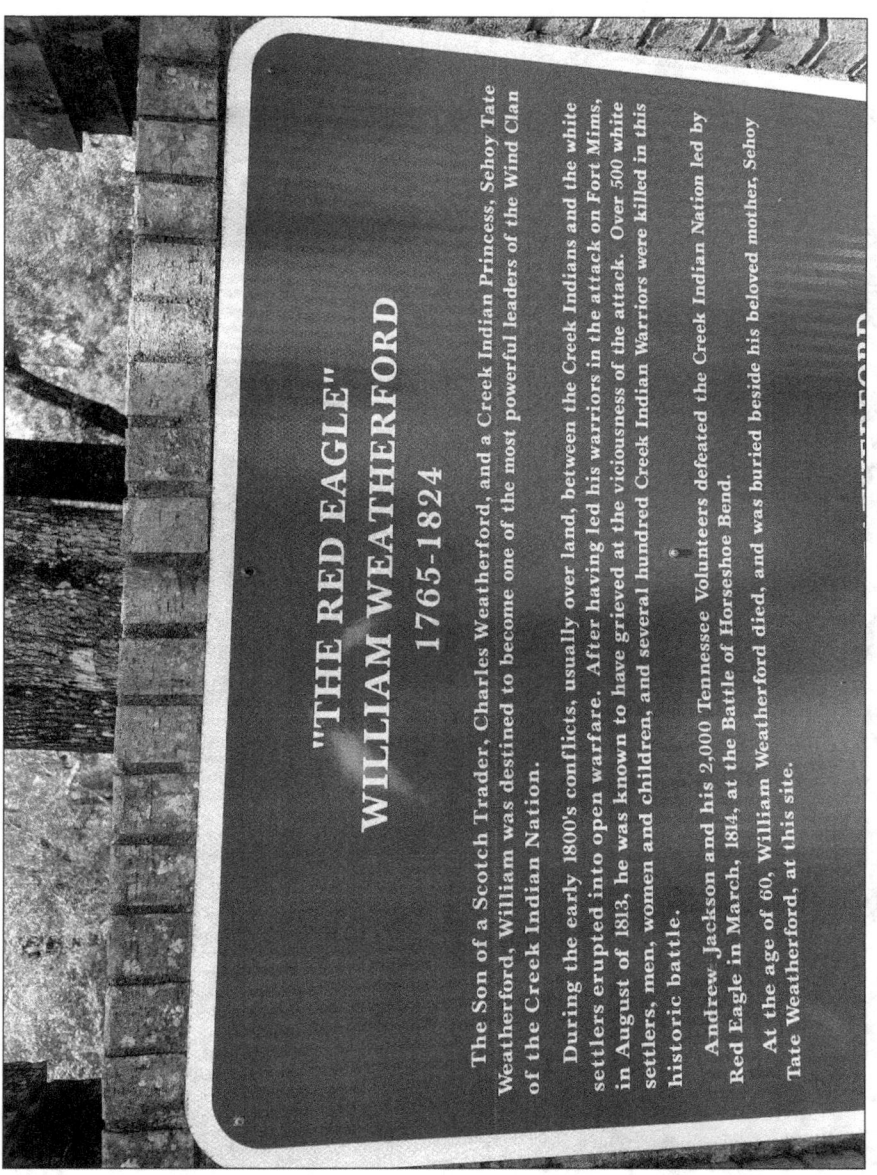

The History of Red Eagle

Holy Ground

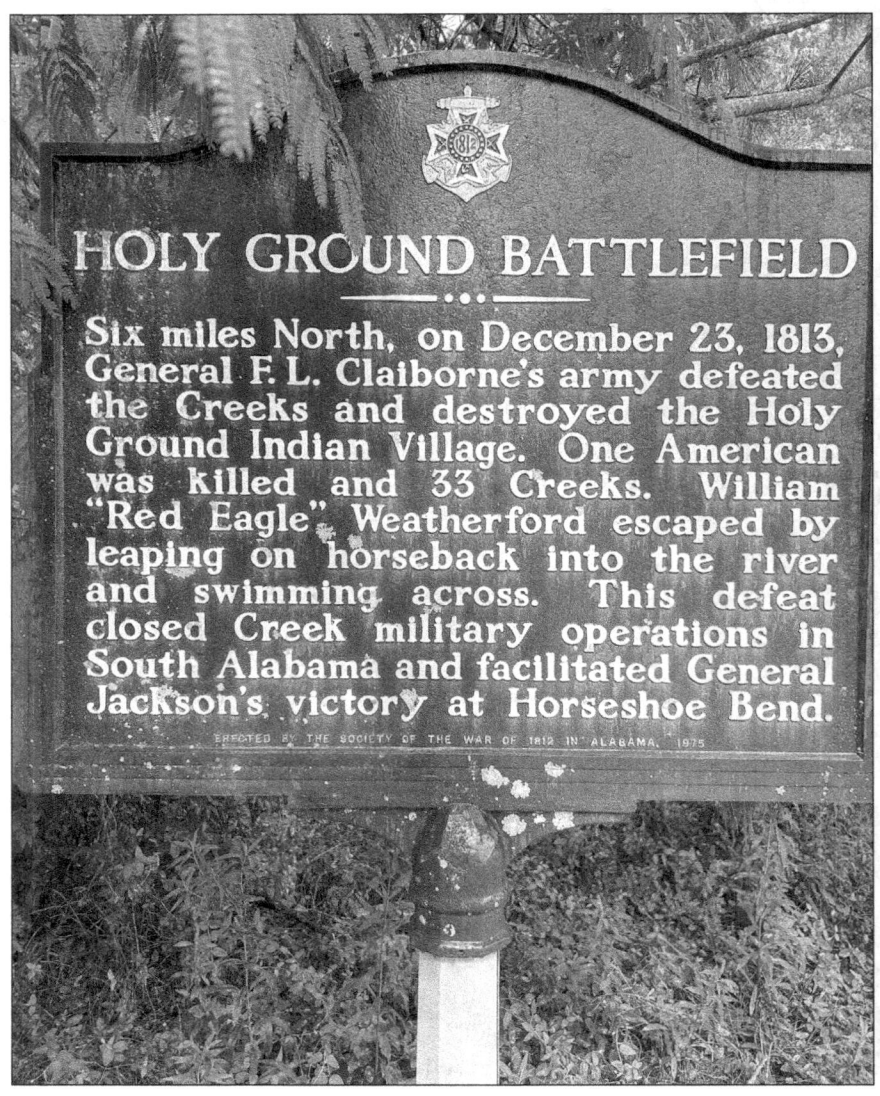

Holy Ground Historic Marker

Author Debra Hughey Stands Near Red Eagle Leaped Into the Alabama River

Red Eagle goes over the bluff at The Battle of Holy Ground.
(Courtesy of The Encyclopedia of Alabama)

Horseshoe Bend

Horsehoe Bend Historic Marker

Cannon at Horseshoe Bend Museum

Entrance to Horseshoe Bend National Military Park

Red Stick Warrior at Barricade at Horseshoe Bend

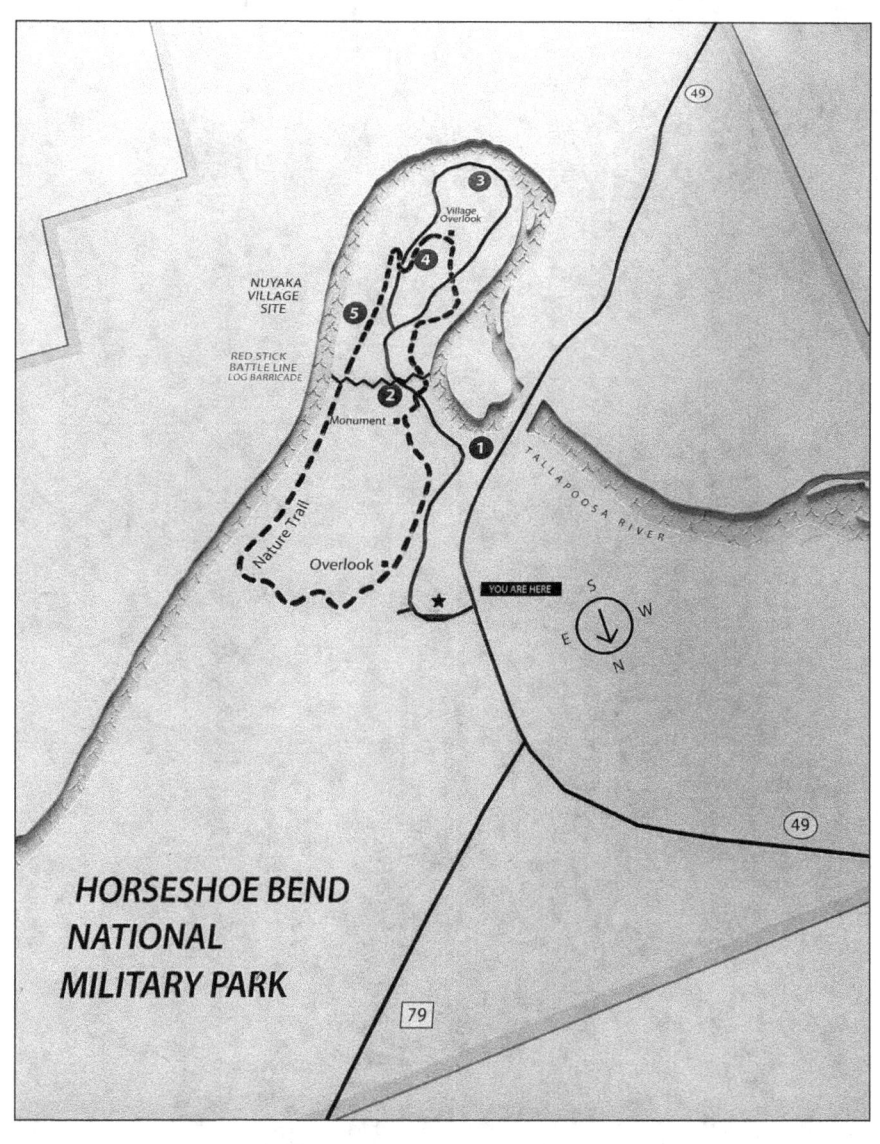

Map of Horseshoe Bend

The Battle of Horseshoe Bend
MARCH 27, 1814

This quiet, secluded spot on the Tallapoosa River was the scene of a fierce battle between Red Stick Creek warriors and US troops and their Indian allies. This decisive battle was the last major engagement of the Creek War of 1813-14.

Creek people from six towns took refuge here during the war. Known as Red Stick Creeks, they constructed a defensive barricade across the peninsula. On March 27, 1814, United States forces, including their Creek and Cherokee allies, attacked.

Never before or since in US history have so many American Indians lost their lives in a single battle. The war had significant consequences for the Creek Nation, the Cherokee Nation, and the US that are still evident today.

Since the 1950s, Horseshoe Bend National Military Park has been protected by the National Park Service and memorialized in partnership with the Muscogee (Creek) Nation in Oklahoma, the Poarch Band of Creek Indians in Alabama, and other affiliated tribal governments.

The Story of Horseshoe Bend

Model of Tohopeka Village

Sticks Used in Stick Ball Game

White Post Showing Where Barricade Stretched Across the Horseshoe of the Tallapoosa River

Tallapoosa River at Tohopeka Village

Weatherford Surrenders to Andrew Jackson (Courtesy of the Museum of the City of Mobile)

Entrance to Fort Toulouse-Fort Jackson

Monument at Fort Toulouse

General Jackson Stone Marker at Ft. Toulouse-Ft. Jackson

Reproduction of Fort Toulouse-Fort Jackson

Site of Fort Toulouse-Fort Jackson

Talisi-Tuckabatchee

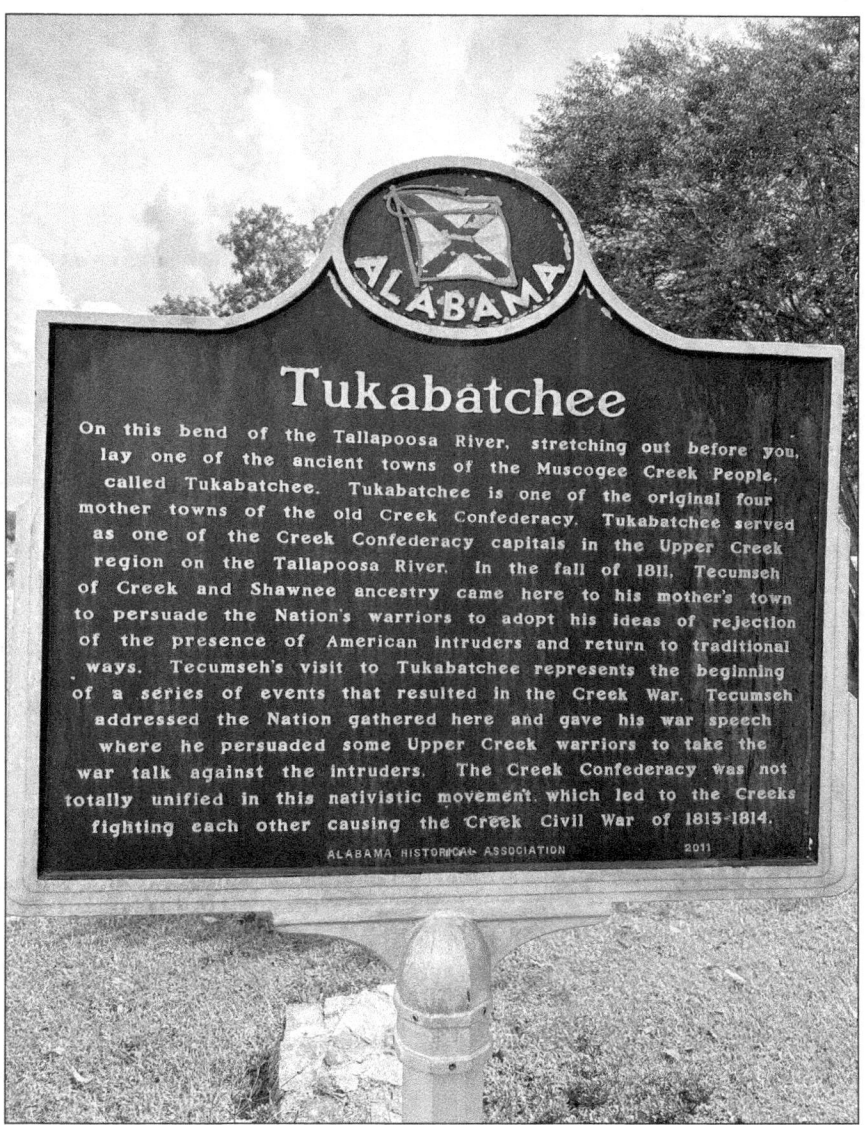

Tuckabatchee Historical Marker

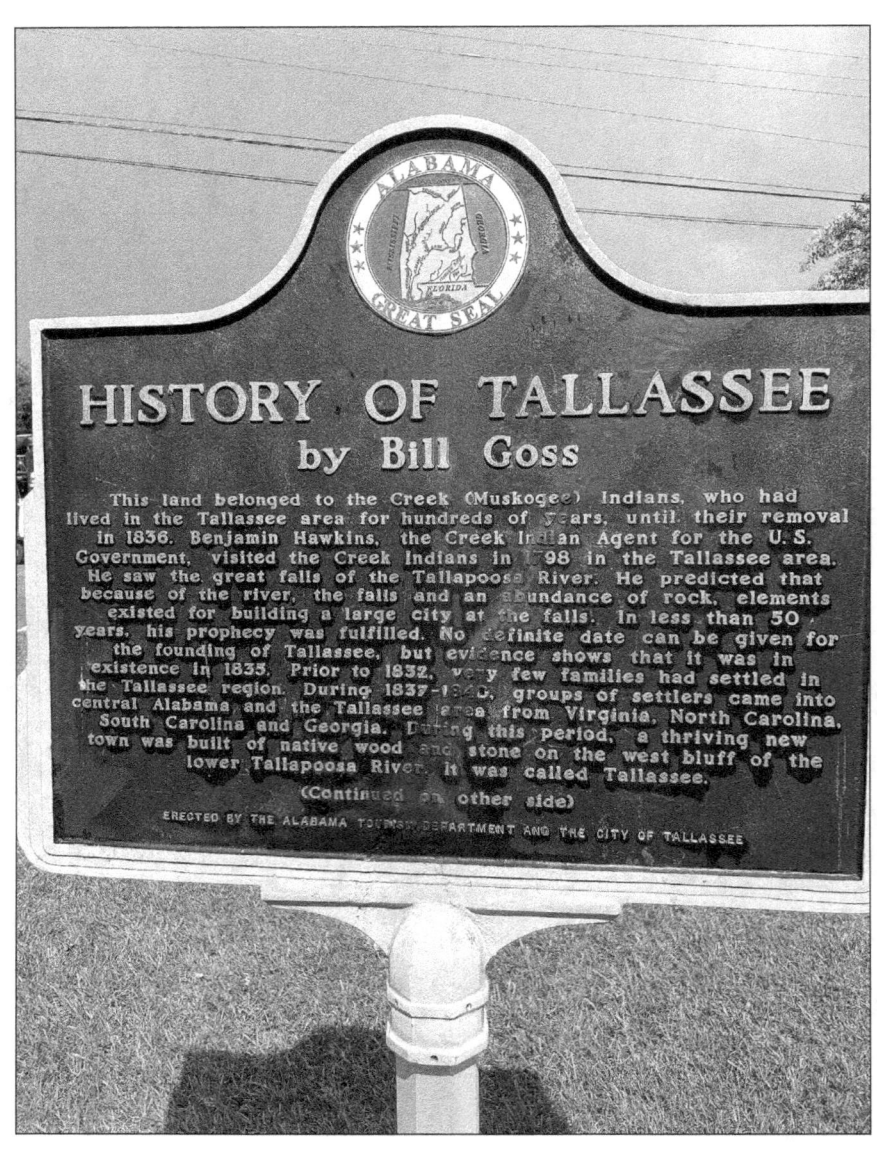

Tallassee Historical Marker

Osceola Monument Next to Tallassee City Hall

*Great Tuckabatchee Council Tree Monument
at Tallassee City Hall*

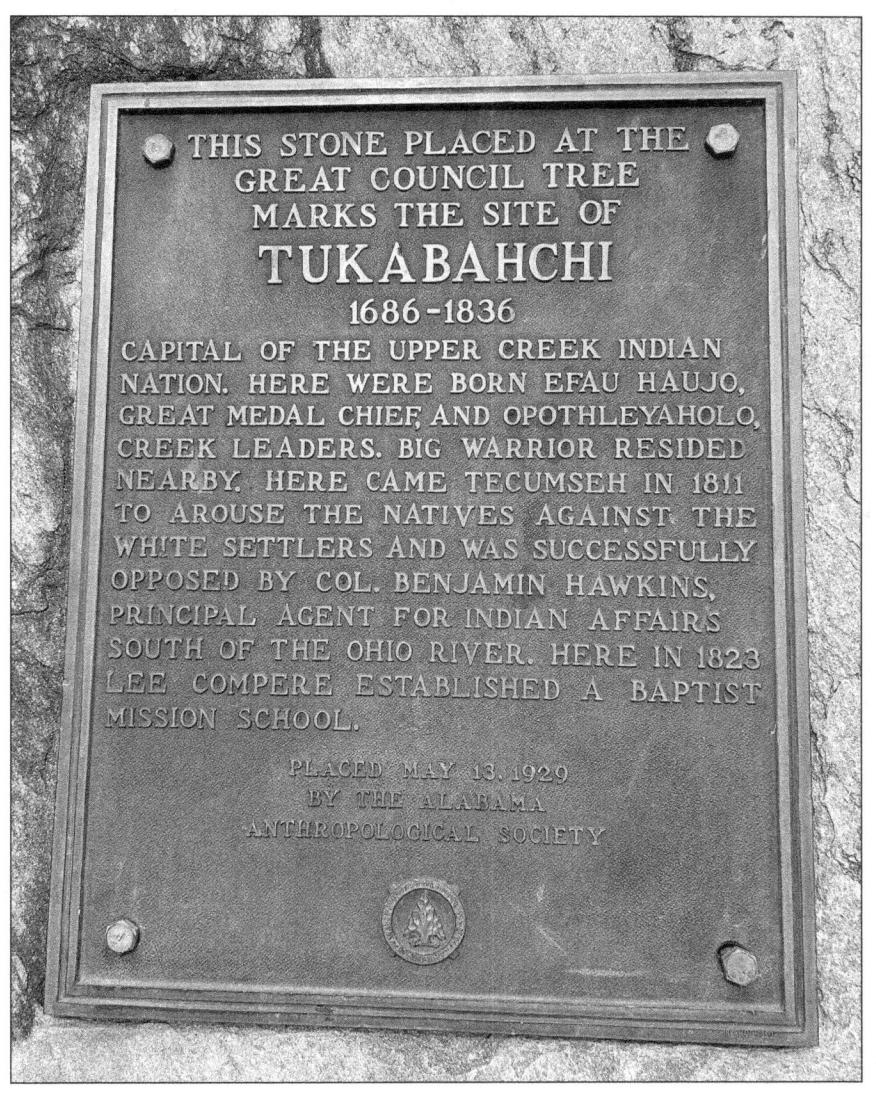

Great Tuckabatchee Council Tree Plaque

Acknowledgments

The Creek War of 1813 and 1814
H.S. Halbert and T.H. Ball

Woodward's Reminiscences of the Creek, or Muscogee Indians
Thomas S. Woodward

Alabama Creek Indians
Lou Vickory

In Bitterness and Tears, Andrew Jackson's Destruction of the Creeks and Seminoles
Sean Michael O'Brien

Tecumseh, A Life
John Sugden

*Red Eagle
And The Wars With The Creek Indians of Alabama
1812-1814*
George C. Eggleston

Photographs

Fort Mims, William Weatherford Monument, Burnt Corn, Holy Ground, Horseshoe Bend, Fort Toulouse, Tuckabatchee and Talisi
Fred Randall Hughey

Front Cover Photograph
Red Eagle Grave Marker at William Weatherford Monument

Back Cover Photograph
The author Debra Hughey standing next to Red Eagle grave marker at William Weatherford Monument

Editing

A big thank you to my husband, Fred Randall Hughey, who gave so much of his time, both in typing, editing and for traveling all over the State of Alabama to secure photos for *The Cry of the Eagle*.

Thank You Sweetheart!

Other Books by Debra Hughey

People of the Townhouse

The Owl and Horseshoe

Spirit of the Red Stick Women

Just A Cotton Field

Dance With The Spirits

Whispering Cedars

**To Order Call 1-888-531-1592
or e-mail wacq@wacqradio.com**

www.ingramcontent.com/pod-product-compliance
Lightning Source LLC
Chambersburg PA
CBHW070106080526
44586CB00013B/1209